Exploring Outdoors Ages 3–11

Exploring Outdoors Ages 3–11 is an essential guide on how to encourage children's learning and support their development through year-round outdoor exploration. It follows one primary school through an entire academic year, capturing the challenges, discoveries and joys of children and adults co-exploring outdoors together.

This unique book covers all aspects of outdoor practice from setting up and maintaining an outdoor site to the support and effective communication needed to create a safe and happy environment. It follows each term of the school year and focuses on the importance of role play and imaginative learning, planning activities for all weather conditions and how the National Curriculum can be applied to outdoor exploring. Features include:

- step-by-step guides on how to set up an outdoor site;
- advice on how to observe and record children's learning and development outdoors;
- real-life case studies of children exploring outdoors from EYFS through to the end of Key Stage 2;
- over 100 photographs to illustrate how outdoor exploring can encourage children's learning and development;
- practical tips and ideas for outdoor activities throughout the year;
- an eResource with useful checklists, templates and pro-forma available to download.

Exploring Outdoors Ages 3–11 is essential reading for school staff who want to build confidence and develop their ability to co-explore outdoors with children.

Helen Bilton PhD is Associate Professor in Education at the University of Reading, UK, and a National Teaching Fellow.

Anne Crook PhD is the Educational Development Consultant (Sciences) at Oxford University, UK, and a National Teaching Fellow.

Exploring Outdoors Ages 3–11

A guide for schools

Helen Bilton and Anne Crook

Waterford City and County
Libraries

Routledge
Taylor & Francis Group

LONDON AND NEW YORK

First published 2016
by Routledge
2 Park Square, Milton Park, Abingdon, Oxon OX14 4RN

and by Routledge
711 Third Avenue, New York, NY 10017

Routledge is an imprint of the Taylor & Francis Group, an informa business

British Library Cataloguing in Publication Data
A catalogue record for this book is available from the British Library

Library of Congress Cataloging in Publication Data
Names: Bilton, Helen, author. | Crook, Anne (Anne C.), author.
Title: Exploring outdoors ages 3–11 : a guide for schools / Helen Bilton and Anne Crook.
Description: Abingdon, Oxon : New York, NY : Routledge, 2016. | Includes bibliographical references and index.
Identifiers: LCCN 2015027667| ISBN 9781138813762 (hbk) | ISBN 9781138814035 (pbk) | ISBN 9781315747774 (ebk)
Subjects: LCSH: Outdoor education. | Outdoor recreation for children. | Education, Elementary.
Classification: LCC LB1047 .B497 2016 | DDC 371.3/84—dc23LC record available at http://lccn.loc.gov/2015027667

ISBN: 978-1-138-81376-2 (hbk)
ISBN: 978-1-138-81403-5 (pbk)
ISBN: 978-1-315-74777-4 (ebk)

Typeset in Bembo
by FiSH Books Ltd, Enfield

MIX
Paper from
responsible sources
FSC   FSC® C013056
www.fsc.org

Printed and bound in Great Britain by
TJ International Ltd, Padstow, Cornwall

For my own family of explorers: Mum, Dad, Rob and Adam. Thank you for everything.

Anne.

Contents

Tables

Acknowledgements

This book came about because of the practice at one school, whose head teacher is passionate about ensuring all children reach their full potential. The school is Chilton Primary School in Oxfordshire, UK, and the head teacher is Sandra North. Sandra believes that children can be helped on their journey of learning by enabling them to regularly explore and work outside, with this outdoor experience being an integral part of the day and curriculum, not as an optional extra. Sandra wants to ensure every child is emotionally and socially strong as well as cognitively and linguistically able and she feels working outside can help children to achieve this.

As a teacher and head teacher Sandra has extensive experience working outside with children. And this, we think, is significant – she has seen both the power of being outside for children and has also learnt to trust the outside as an influential learning environment. She has first-hand experience not only of the long-term impact of outdoor residential trips, but also the effect of having outside trails, orienteering, digging, and pond explorations available to children as a regular part of their school week. Children working and learning outside is a core part of the school's ethos. Sandra's love of the outdoors began as a child. Sandra's parents were from the east end of London but moved to the outskirts of London when she was young. Walking was one of the family traditions, on Sundays travelling to Southend to walk on the beach. All the family had walking shoes and her brother was a 'bit of an ornithologist'. She still walks and finds it an important way to de-stress.

Sandra says it is not easy having a child-friendly, curriculum-linked outdoor area, offering exciting experiences all year round. It needs to be created in the first place, but then tended and cared for, so it remains a sustainable site. Thanks to the efforts of Sandra, the staff and school volunteers, the outdoor area now comprises a small patch of woodland, a pond, hills and felled trees for the children to explore. There is also a well-tended allotment, which enables the children to grow their own fruit and vegetables. Through being outdoors in these spaces the children have opportunities to experience being ecological explorers in the woodland area, recreate battles from history and scenes from Shakespeare or conduct scientific experiments. Sandra and her staff have seen that quiet children can become more confident outside and when they are together in this environment, children are observed to work collaboratively, sometimes in ways that they do not achieve in class. Outside children can also just be children.

Sandra is a head teacher with a vision and is aware that you need to take people with you if you are to realise your ambitions. The regular outdoor explorations that the children experience would not be possible without the full commitment of the staff and school volunteers. Parents also need to be on board and Sandra and her staff have worked hard to ensure that the outdoor learning approach is embedded within school practice. For example, all the children are expected to have wellington boots and weather appropriate clothing in school every day. Parents therefore expect children to be working outside year-round. The school is able to show that the children who have experienced outdoor explorations have become resilient against the weather and more interested in nature. But the proof of the outdoor approach, Sandra suggests, is with the children who then take home that love of the outside and teach their families about it. They demonstrate their excitement about being outdoors and become the ambassadors for this approach to learning.

Our heartfelt thanks go to Sandra North and all the staff and children at Chilton Primary School for allowing us to play a part in your outdoor explorations.

Introduction

Figure 11.0 Den building is a common activity when children are given the freedom to explore outdoors

Why have we written this book and why should you read it?

This book is for everyone. And we mean everyone. Whether you like being outdoors or not and whether you like your children being outdoors or not. And it is definitely not just for those already converted to the benefits of the outdoor environment. Our aim is that by the time you have finished this book you will either be affirmed in what you already know (and we all need affirmation), you will have greater knowledge and confidence to further develop outdoor learning in your own school or you will be a convert and have already gone out and bought the right clothing to start exploring outdoors. So what do we mean by outdoor exploration? What we do not mean is playing outside with plastic toys or indoor games being played outdoors. We are talking about children's engagement with the natural environment using minimal man-made resources. We mean experiencing outside whatever the weather, where adults and children are exploring and learning together.

What is so special about outdoor exploration?

There is something special about being outdoors. From our perspective many of our fondest and most detailed childhood memories stem from exploring the natural world on our own, or co-exploring with family and friends. When we are both doing our predominantly indoor day job we often find ourselves looking out the window wishing we were outside – even on wet days. Now you may say, "*Well, that's just you, I don't feel like that, especially in cold, wet weather*" but we would say that you too recognise that being outdoors is actually rather special, even if you do not necessarily share our enthusiasm for inclement weather. For example, take our foraging metaphor. We are fortunate enough to live in the developed world where having enough food to eat is not a problem and we therefore have no need to go outdoors to forage in search of food. But have you been outdoors and explored your local hedgerows, woods or forests in search of food, like edible fruits? Think back to how it felt to find the fruit, to pick it and then to eat it outdoors, there and then. These sorts of experience provide you with an engagement with the natural world that buying the same fruit in a shop just cannot give you – although we agree that the latter method maybe a more convenient way of obtaining the fruit!

We would go further and say, not only can experiences be different outdoors, they can be richer and so can the learning that takes place alongside them (Bilton (2010), Dillon, Morris, O'Donnell, Reid, Rickinson, and Scott (2005) and Muñoz, (2009). Not even the most complex computer programme or high quality TV documentary can provide you with the complexity of sounds, sights, smells, tastes and textures of exploring the natural world. Put simply, if you really want to explore the outdoors, you do physically have to go outside and experience it for yourself. We realise that this is a rather obvious statement; however, if you bear in mind the technological advances that have taken place in recent years and how much information is now available to many children at the touch of a button thanks to ever more sophisticated smartphones and tablet computers, we as teachers, teaching assistants and parents have an enormous responsibility to ensure that children grow up understanding that a computer game or TV programme about outdoor exploration will *never* be the same as doing the exploring yourself.

Many children, of course, do not need to be told how to explore outdoors – take them outside and present them with a tree possessing a curvy branch and they will turn the branch into a swing (see Figure I1.1) or a place to hang from (see Figure I1.2). Others will have

Figure 11.1 Children make use of natural resources in a range of ways. Here a curved branch is turned into a swing for a group of Key Stage 1 children

Figure 11.2 The same curved branch is used here by a pair of Key Stage 2 children as a place from which to hang upside-down

extreme confidence in being outdoors, jumping from logs and trees with ease (see Figure I1.3). Similarly, show a child a puddle and many will happily wade in, sometimes only realising too late that their wellington boots are just about to fill with water (see Figure I1.4). We do, however, recognise that not all children (or indeed adults) possess this confidence and/or interest in exploring outdoors!

Figure I1.3 Some children are naturally confident in climbing and jumping

Figure I1.4 Puddles are a source of fascination for many children when exploring outdoors

Aims of this book

This book aims to provide you with the need to know information to both help support your first journeys in outdoor exploration with children and to help maintain the momentum for those of you who are already doing it with children ranging in age from early years, EYFS (nursery) through to primary Key Stage 1 and 2, that is ages three through to eleven. We aim to show you the importance of taking children outdoors to explore the natural world in terms of the learning and developmental opportunities it can provide. We also hope to share with you our belief that working with children outdoors in a natural environment can lead to open-ended tandem learning journeys for both the children and participating adults, i.e. co-exploration, with a wide range of potential learning outcomes, but also linked back to learning inside. In this way, outdoor exploration becomes even more distinct from an indoor classroom setting in which the adults are often seen as the experts who lead the children through scheduled learning pathways with (generally) pre-determined end points and outcomes.

How to use this book

We have spent many years exploring the natural world with children and we know that you know your children best. So this is not a book that will tell you how you should do things. Instead, think of it as a pragmatic handbook to support your ideas and/or to give you some food for thought to help you and your children maximise the potential of outdoor exploration within your own school context. We have therefore written it to cater both for those of you who may be starting outdoor exploration for the first time as well as for those of you who are more experienced in working outdoors with children and may already have an established outdoor site.

Over the course of one academic year we kept diaries which included detailed observations, quotes, reflections and photographs from each weekly outdoor exploring session that we led in one primary school in the UK. These provided us with a rich source of information, which we have drawn on extensively throughout the book. In this way we show how we put into practice everything which is detailed in this book in our own outdoor explorer sessions with children.

The book is divided into three sections. Section I covers the basic need to know information to help support the adults who are leading and/or supporting outdoor work with children (Chapter 1), the knowledge to get the most from children when working outside (Chapter 2) and an overview of things to consider when setting up a site for outdoor exploration (Chapter 3). These three chapters are based on our own experiences that either starting from scratch or even developing an existing programme of outdoor exploration within an early years/primary school setting can have many challenges. Section I therefore provides guidance on how to avoid or deal with the most common of these, based both on our collective experiences and from established research evidence in this area.

Section II of the book covers an academic year in the life of a UK primary school engaged in a range of outdoor explorations with children aged from early years (nursery) through to Key Stage 2. These chapters share the experiences of the children and adults and provide insight into the impact that outdoor exploration has on learning and development through inclusion of detailed case studies based on real-life events. This makes our book unique because it shares with you a living experience of exploring outdoors with children at one site over an extended period of time. For convenience the chapters within Section II are organised across three academic term-based themes: autumn–winter term (Chapter 4); winter–spring term (Chapter 5) and spring–summer term (Chapter 6). Although these three chapters are set within a primary school in Oxfordshire in the UK does that mean it is only relevant to similar schools? We don't think so because we have had so many discussions about so many issues over the years and we have considered these from so many angles that we believe you will find inspiration for your school or setting in any country. That said, every country will, of course, have its own weather patterns and the weather is a hugely important factor that you will have to take into consideration when working outdoors with children. Once you know your weather for your setting though we are confident that you will be able to make use of the principles inherent in this book irrespective of where you are based in the world.

Section III is the main resource section and comprises a variety of information ranging from relevant educational literature, pro-forma, templates, checklists, where to source handy outdoor resources and a list of useful websites and other online resources.

The book can therefore be read in a linear fashion from the basics outlined in Section I through to the real life case studies covered in Section II, or it can be used as a reference book to dip in and out of to suit your needs. Either way we anticipate there is something in this book for everyone, irrespective of your level of experience in working outdoors with children. Above all else we hope that by reading this book we can help develop your confidence in leading and/or supporting outdoor explorations with your children. Our firm belief is that confident adults equipped with the right frame of mind for working outdoors with children can help set the scene for some of the most important learning experiences that children may have at school. So, we therefore start in the first chapter with the adults and the pivotal role they play in shaping outdoor exploration.

Section I

The following three chapters focus on the need to know information to help you set up or develop further your outdoor explorations with early years/primary-aged children. This information is based on our collective experience of working with children and adults over a number of years and across a range of early years and primary school settings. In Chapter 1, we focus on the pivotal role of the adults in leading and/or supporting children's outdoor explorations. How to work effectively with children, observing and supporting learning is covered in Chapter 2. Chapter 3 then provides an essential guide to planning, setting up and sustaining your outdoor site.

Adults who show an active interest in being outdoors are key to the success of a programme of outdoor exploration

Appropriate clothing and a caring attitude towards children when working outdoors is essential

Children can create quite complex play scenarios using only natural resources

Working with children outdoors provides opportunities for rich conversations

Children learn to work together to be creative and to solve problems when provided with a range of natural materials outdoors

Chapter 1

Outdoor exploration starts with the adults

Figure 1.0 Children working as a team outdoors

This chapter covers the role of adults in supporting outdoor explorations. We start with this topic because the adults involved in your outdoor sessions have a pivotal role to play. In particular, in terms of setting an appropriate example to children and in supporting you to help children gain the most from their outdoor experiences. Your success in outdoor explorations really does depend on the work you put in to support your adult helpers and colleagues and the ways in which you communicate with the parents/carers of the children in your group.

This chapter therefore starts with the key elements to think about in relation to effective adult support for your outdoor sessions, which then leads into the ways in which you can foster successful lines of communication with the parents/carers of your children.

Attitude

In a nutshell, adults' attitudes are hugely influential in setting an appropriate example for children as they prepare to go outdoors. Of course, chances are at some point during the year there will be inclement weather; for example, heavy rain, wind, possibly even snow and ice depending on where your school is located. So you will need to be prepared to go outdoors in pretty much all weathers to run a year-long programme of outdoor exploration and to help children appreciate the seasonal changes in the weather and how to deal with these (see Figure 1.1).

In our experience adults who are not bothered by the weather (or at least they do not overtly show it), who are calm, confident, suitably dressed for the local weather and enthusiastic, will help create an environment in which children feel safe and more relaxed about going outdoors in all weathers themselves. The converse is also true. Adults who fuss around children, who overtly express a desire to stay clean and dry, who appear to be anxious and/or are themselves inappropriately dressed for the weather conditions are sending out a message to the children that effectively says *"I'm not going to enjoy this and neither are you, so let's just get it over and done with as quickly as possible"*. The adult with responsibility for leading outdoor sessions therefore has a key role to play in communicating expectations amongst both teaching colleagues and the other supporting adults. We appreciate, of course, that mustering the enthusiasm amongst adults to take a group of children to explore outdoors on a wet, windy,

Figure 1.1 An outdoor session leader helping a child put on his gloves in preparation for an exploring session in the winter

cold November day can be challenging. But it can be done. For example, by giving the children and adults a treat to look forward to during the session, such as a drink of hot chocolate and a snack; by starting the session off encouraging everyone to work together to build a shelter; or by incorporating some fun physical exercises to keep everyone active and warm, like a game of tag or hide and seek. And after all that, just think how much more you will appreciate being outdoors when the more pleasant spring weather arrives! As one of our field diary entries illustrates:

> *"The session today felt really different to the last time I had this Key Stage 2 group. Last time we were together the weather was horrible and some of the children got really cold and miserable and we ended up curtailing the session as a result. This time the weather was a bit better and all of the children moaned when we had to go back into class. Our explorer sessions show, through experience, how much the weather can influence how we feel about being outdoors and also how important it is to be appropriately dressed and prepared for outdoor exploration. I think the previous cold, wet session was a real eye-opener for some of the children who I don't think had spent an extended period of time outdoors in that sort of weather before."*

By experiencing poorer weather it enables us to appreciate the better weather and to learn that we are able to cope in all weathers.

Figure 1.2 is the transcript of a conversation with a teaching assistant who went from being more of a fair-weather outdoor person to a very strong advocate of all-weather outdoor exploration through working with us and a group of Year 4 children over a three-month period.

"I was asked if I could help Anne on the outdoor exploring sessions. All through the winter, prior to starting to help, I was not looking forward to being outside, I didn't like being outside. I am much more of an indoor person. Or so I thought. Then on my first day of outdoor explorers I was bad tempered and grumpy. It was pouring down with rain, it was cold. I didn't enjoy the session at all.

However, as the weeks went by my attitude started to change. This began with the simple task of checking the weather forecast and when it said it was poor and cold weather I just put more layers on. I know it's not rocket science but I found the more layers you wear the warmer you stay! I got to the point after a few outdoor explorer sessions of not caring about the wet or inclement weather, it wasn't a problem. I can remember saying to Anne: 'I'm not an outdoor type of girl and explorers is really taking me out of my comfort zone, but do you know what, I'm really enjoying it!' No one was more surprised than me about this!

Then I really surprised my husband, who loves being outside, by suggesting we went for a walk! And in the rain! And I still like going for walks and being outside.

I have learnt that it isn't the end of the world if we get wet, there are spare clothes, and you simply have to become rain - proofed to the weather. Being outside teaches you how to be equipped for all weather scenarios.

I was really sad when outdoor explorers with Anne had finished. I was shocked how much I got from it, how much benefit there was".

Figure 1.2 The transcript of a conversation with a teaching assistant who went from being more of a fair-weather outdoor person to a very strong advocate of all-weather outdoor exploration

Having continuity of staff

It helps to have the same adult helpers every week wherever possible. They get to know your expectations and they gain important knowledge about the children which can be fed back to the classroom teachers. It also gives you security as the session leader, as highlighted in one of our field diary entries.

"It was really helpful having the Year 4 teaching assistant available to help with the outdoor sessions as she had in-depth knowledge of the children. I felt much happier knowing I was going to have this same dedicated helper each week, thus enabling me to build up a working relationship with her. In other year groups I've worked with outdoors I'd always found it quite stressful not knowing from one week to the next who would be coming out to help me".

This was followed up a few weeks later by this diary comment:

"Having the same adult helpers each week has enabled me to build a really good rapport with them. We now work as a team, knowing when to get snacks ready, when to round up the children to wash their hands and when to step back and allow children the freedom to enjoy exploring the site".

In terms of expectations you will want to allow the children freedom to explore. They can only do this if the adults are relaxed, as illustrated in this diary entry:

"It was important to me to come across as a relaxed, confident leader and I think I achieved this....I wanted to make sure that the session was more or less child-led and that as adults we stepped back as much as possible and allowed the children to sort out any issues that might arise e.g. disputes over sharing of resources. We let the children resolve their problems whilst we observed from a distance. I think this is hugely important. We must intervene, of course, if things look like they might get out of hand, but learning to sort disagreements out and cope with things not going your way is an important outcome of the sessions as far as I am concerned. It's also a significant contribution to a child's holistic development".

This approach can only really happen if one knows the adults working with you and they understand this approach.

Helpers can be anxious

If the teachers/teaching assistants and parents are happy about children exploring outside then this usually means the children will be too. At the start of the new academic year, you may find you have to re-establish your ways of working which you thought were fully embedded when you finished for the annual break. Parents and adult helpers may once again be anxious and you need to give them security in the ways in which you run your outdoor sessions. This was just the case with one parent helper in the autumn term as this diary entry highlights:

"One thing I found hard to deal with today was when one of the parent helpers was hovering around the children as they climbed on and off the piles of logs in the woodland area. I felt that by continually offering a hand for the children to hold the parent wasn't encouraging the children to

challenge themselves. When an opportune time arose I quietly suggested to the parent that it was ok to step back and to only provide support if the children asked for assistance. I was relieved (if I'm being really honest!) that only one of the 10 children climbing at the time asked for help. The other children appeared delighted to have been given free rein to jump and climb".

Pretend gun play or play fighting can be an issue for some adults (see Chapter 5) but as long as it is managed appropriately then there should be no problem. We have experienced some difference of opinion on this, as shown in the following diary entry:

"The children used sticks to play various gun games today. During the session I heard one of the adult helpers say very loudly "No guns boys, this is explorers group!" I don't know where this helper got that idea from. As session leader I don't mind if the children play games with sticks as long as they look out for themselves and other people when playing. The children know this because one of our explorer rules is to look after each other when exploring and playing outside".

One has to be aware that there is play fighting, which is rough and tumble, and real fighting, which is aggression. The majority of children know the difference; however adults without closely observing what is going on, can sometimes jump in with both feet and demand a cessation to the activity, unaware children are simply play fighting. Blurton-Jones (1967, p.355) identified seven stages to play fighting: running, chasing and felling, wrestling, jumping up and down with both feet together, beating at each other with an open hand without actually hitting, beating at each other with an object but not hitting and laughing. Play fighting is often a part of superhero play, something which should be accessible to both boys and girls. A hugely significant book on this subject is by Penny Holland (2003) and in her research she found that banning gun play does not solve anything and children end up play fighting on the hoof and in secret. However, in those settings where superhero play was allowed, the actual construction of the guns became more complicated and an occupation in itself. Children who do show a tendency toward more violent play themes will not stop simply by banning play fighting. Rather those children need lots of adult guidance, support and help to rehabilitate them back into playing appropriately with others. So rather than ban play fighting, ensure you discuss with all adults your reasoning behind allowing it and the rules regarding safe play fighting. Also ensure the children know how to behave appropriately so that no child feels actually in danger, ensuring children are careful not to wave pointed objects near eyes and the children know if someone says "stop" or "go away" or "I don't like that", then they do stop.

Who should help?

You have to be really thoughtful about who helps you and consider both their motivation for helping and who is gaining, or not, from their involvement, as this diary entry illustrates:

"I think it can be problematic having the parent/family member of one of your children helping at a session as it's really hard not to go into protective mum mode. I certainly know from first-hand experience that it's not easy! A diplomatic strategy works well so that you don't upset the adult – you need to be aware that they're giving up their time to help – but at the same time parent volunteers need to respect the ethos of your sessions. Many children are very well equipped to assess different risks, including whether or not they feel comfortable to climb/jump onto a log. But if mum, dad or grandma is there, the opportunity for a child to assess risk themselves might be lost".

It is a case of making the adult helpers aware of your philosophy and approach and confident to be a part of it. Make sure you know why you are doing things as you are, so that you can carefully explain the benefits of this approach to the parents/family members of the children in your care. In this way adult helpers can be convinced the approach will benefit the children, as the following diary extract highlights:

> "One of the parents came out with me today and commented several times in the session that she thought she'd need eyes in the back of her head being with such young children outdoors (the group comprised three and four year olds). However, at the end of the session she said the children were actually really sensible and not at all what she had expected!"

Wiping the slate clean

When you teach and/or support children in a typical indoor classroom setting you naturally build up a profile of each individual child: what they do and do not enjoy doing; what they excel at; what they find challenging; how they behave in different scenarios; how they interact with their peers and with adults. For us, an important component of regularly working with children outdoors is being prepared to temporarily park these profiles each time you step outside with your group. In other words be prepared to wipe the slate clean and see your children in a new light when they are exploring outdoors. This means being prepared to be amazed and/or surprised by how the children adapt, play, explore and behave outdoors. Above all we think you should not necessarily expect a child's indoor profile to be replicated in a natural outdoor setting. We do, however, appreciate that this is much easier said than done, we are only human after all. However, if you and the other adults at least aim to start each outdoor session with a blank slate for each child, the chances are you may well observe something that perhaps you might otherwise have missed because of your pre-existing knowledge of that child. This can be especially important for children who may find indoor classroom learning particularly challenging, whereas within an outdoor setting these children may find avenues in which to shine. This is highlighted in the following diary entry:

> "There was a new member in today's Year 6 explorers group who had recently joined the school, so I took the opportunity to go over and introduce myself and to find out a bit more about him. Totally unprompted he started to talk to me about his behaviour in school; he said he didn't always concentrate in class and that he had sometimes got into trouble at his last school. He also said "I'm not very clever". He looked quite sad when I said it must be hard being the new person in the class when everyone else has known each other for years. To lighten the mood I asked him about his hobbies. His face lit up as he told me about the things he does outdoors with his family. We chatted about looking after the environment and it was clear to me that he had a really good knowledge of natural history. Shortly after I had left to go and see some of the other children he climbed one of the nearby trees and sat looking out over the school playing field. Some of the other boys in the group had been watching us and were clearly impressed at how quickly he'd climbed the tree; they then tried to climb the same tree but without much success. It was immediately apparent to me that this was an important moment for the new member of the group – the tree climbing was something he could easily do that the other children were not yet quite as good at. I saw this as a levelling moment and I don't believe it would have happened if the children had not been outdoors exploring that day".

Of course the converse may also be true. Children who excel within a highly structured, adult-led classroom environment may find a less predictable, predominantly child-led outdoor explorers session more challenging. An example of this is shown through the following diary extract:

> "One of the Key Stage 2 children complained of having cold feet part way through the session today, so I suggested ways she could help herself to warm up, like running on the spot, doing star jumps, running around the site and so on. A few minutes later this same child (whom, I was informed, is normally very diligent in class) said to one of the adults "I'm bored, I don't know what to do". Rather than suggesting things she could do, the adult commented on what the other children were doing, then left her to her own devices to have some thinking time. A few minutes later this same child collected a pair of sticks of roughly the same length and was observed pretending to be cross-country ski-ing on one of the frosty wooden sleepers. She was fully engrossed in this activity for quite some time and by the huge smile on her face, was clearly enjoying the fact that she'd made up this activity all by herself".

So, it is important to be prepared for these sorts of scenarios where children may take naturally to outdoor exploring, whereas others may need more time and support outdoors to motivate, enthuse and build their confidence over time.

Co-exploring

In order to fully embrace what we see as an important component of outdoor exploration, namely co-exploration, you need to leave the formal instructive style of teaching at the door. In other words if you want to transform your outdoor sessions into genuine opportunities for co-exploration it is really important that you too are actively engaged in learning alongside your children, i.e. you are no longer the sole leader/teacher/expert. This does not, of course, mean that you have to leave behind all your knowledge and experience of the outdoors or indeed that your sessions have to be unstructured *per se*. It does, however, require you to be confident enough to step back and allow the children to have opportunities to dictate the nature and pace of the session within your pre-determined safety boundaries. You then use your knowledge and experience to decide when to step-in, for example, in helping children to learn how to identify a particular animal or plant that has taken their interest if they don't already know what it is.

Taking children outdoors and providing them with more freedom than perhaps they may be used to experiencing to explore and interact with the natural environment can sometimes, however, be a nerve-wracking business, especially if your knowledge of the children and/or of the site is still under-development or if it is different from other roles you may have in school. A good example of this is highlighted in the following diary entry:

> "One of the teaching assistants mentioned today how being outdoors has shown her that you can have fun if you're properly dressed. She said that she's learning to stand back and observe the children much more through these outdoor exploring sessions, something which she said as a teaching assistant and lunchtime supervisor, she doesn't always feel able to do".

As adults there can be a temptation to want to keep stepping in, to hover around the children and/or to blatantly interfere. As Bruce (2005) discusses, we need to interact not interfere and there is skill in adults learning and then knowing when to do the former and not the latter, with practise improving the skill. However, if you have, or can develop, the confidence to take a step back, to see these outdoor exploration sessions as golden opportunities for children to experience some genuine responsibility; to learn to self-assess risk; to interact appropriately with their peers and their surroundings, you will be helping to build their confidence, equipping them with a huge range of complex lifelong learning skills as well as giving yourself an opportunity to learn more about your children in your outdoor setting. In fact when Year 6 children were asked about their outdoor experiences they said:

> *"it's a different kind of education" and helped them to develop the following skills: "Makes us well rounded; gives us confidence; makes us think logically e.g. the den building; makes you realise what you can do".*

Figure 1.3 shows our examples of learning experienced by children outdoors.

Forming relationships with children

It takes time to form relationships with children and particularly so in an environment children may not be that familiar with. You need to have a clear structure to your sessions even if that is that there is a good deal of freedom! Children cannot guess your philosophy or rules, so they need to be told and regularly reminded (see Section III for our list of explorer rules). So this will involve the way you travel to the site (for example walking in twos holding hands), entering your site via the same place each time, starting the session in the same way and/or in the same place, and the indicator to stop and gather (for example making a noise, like beating a tambourine). The younger the child the more visual cues will be required. For example, Figure 1.4 shows an outdoor session leader making use of pictures to focus children's attention on one of the good listening explorer rules.

Some children will need more cajoling, some may need more initial close contact with you, some may need to be encouraged through role modelling; for example starting a hide and seek game, or collecting leaves to note the range of colours, or collecting sticks to make a den. Where you are trying to take the children in their learning will be based on where they are now and that means some may be have much less knowledge, experience and confidence and so will need this building up over time. It is important to remember that we all need to be given time to get used to anything new. This is particularly pertinent to younger children. For example, give children opportunities to look at insects but not touch them until they are ready. Patience and role modelling are important attributes for you to have. So you then handle the insects, demonstrating how to carefully treat the animal, but also reassuring through action that it is fine to handle them. The following diary entry shows how these sorts of interactions with children can help strengthen relationships with children, as well as providing opportunities to boost children's confidence:

> *"This holding back regarding touching the insects was really common at the start of my work with the younger nursery children. I think it's quite a useful metric of how far children can grow in their confidence by regularly taking part in outdoor explorations; it starts with a reluctance to hold/touch an insect/other mini-beast but then quite quickly over a few weeks the children can be seen to progress through to stages where they are independently finding, holding and showing these animals to their peers and to the adults."*

A list of some of the learning observed during our observations of children exploring outdoors:

- listening, really listening and focussing on the sound or speech for a period of time
- looking, taking time to look and observe and consider and making judgments based on those observations
- explaining where/when/how something happened/occurred, for how long, who was there
- explaining what was done, who was involved
- explaining what something is, how it got there, factors about the animal or plant, living and survival conditions
- understanding and appreciating cause and effect, with for example regards oneself – well wrapped up and you keep warm and regards the environment – don't stamp on insects as they are living creatures
- surviving and triumphing over the weather
- taking risks, and trusting ones own judgement
- getting hurt and knowing how to help oneself and knowing one will get better given time (often). There is a strong belief among many people that one must not get hurt and then if one does the pain/issue cannot last for long – this isn't always the reality
- appreciating that someone else might know something you don't and feeling happy to accept advice and new knowledge from peers
- conquering a fear
- cooperating with others, including leading others, being led by others, and using the language (verbal and body) of cooperation to work together
- willingness to persevere with a project when the obvious solution does not appear
- using ones imagination to design and sustain play situations including the symbolic representation of natural materials
- becoming self-reliant and thereby able to interest oneself
- learning to challenge oneself physically, academically, emotionally
- independent and team based learning
- problem solving – use of mathematical concepts and terminology
- contextualising learning (bringing indoor learning outdoors and vice versa) – learning about colours in class then seeing those (and more!) colours outside, e.g. leaf colour in autumn
- dealing with failure (e.g. den collapsing – wood too heavy) and opportunities to achieve (building den with more appropriate structure)
- learning new skills, e.g. how to use wildlife identification guides
- learning about life and death in nature
- learning about transformations in nature: for example, seeing the development of tadpoles into frogs in the wild, which helps contextualise in-class learning
- observing the seasons and what this means for animals and plants
- learning to respect and care for the environment
- learning wrong from right – it's not ok to step on an insect just because you are physically able to do so etc.

Figure 1.3 A list of examples of learning observed in children exploring outdoors

Figure 1.4 Using pictures to focus children's attention on the outdoor explorer rules

At the start of our outdoor exploring sessions with some three and four-year olds one of the children was observed to lack confidence in getting close to the insects we were discovering. However, within the space of a few weeks and with adult support, this child grew enormously in confidence. Figure 1.5 shows her holding one of her insect discoveries.

Some children's behaviour can decline outside and it may be necessary to develop new strategies to help children focus. For example, we've successfully developed the zip-method of helping children to listen when we're talking outdoors, as noted in this diary entry:

> *"I ask all the children to pretend to have a zip on their mouth and the only time they can talk when we're sat in the log circle is when the lead adult says they can undo their zip and put their hand up to indicate that they want to talk. I tried it today when I was running through our explorer rules and it worked well with those who tend to simply shout out. It also enabled those children who tend to be quiet in a group to contribute".*

This is an accessible and fun way which even young children can grasp.

Figure 1.5 An EYFS child sharing her insect discovery

Risk and challenge, danger and hazard

Children do not need to face danger and hazard but they do need to learn about risk and challenge. In this way we can ensure they become independent and self-sufficient and this keeps them safe. However, it will be the adult who will make an environment challenging and exciting or simple and undemanding. Waller and colleagues demonstrate that we allow risk or not, dependent on our view of the child and whether we view the child 'as competent rather than…as vulnerable and in need of adult protection' (Arlemalm-Hagser, Maynard, Sandseter, Waller & Wyver, 2010, p. 441). We all face challenges and for children this could be about crossing the road or understanding some aspect of maths. Our role as adults is to help children to develop a bank of strategies to help themselves and probably even more importantly trust themselves to make judgements about everything including knowing when it is safe to cross the road and knowing that one can seek help regarding a mathematical problem. The Royal Society for the Prevention of Accidents (RoSPA 2015) and the Health and Safety Executive (HSE 2015), both argue strongly that children need to learn to face and overcome challenges and that risk taking is an important life learning tool. Indeed RoSPA talk about the need for children to have safety and risk education and the importance of it. We hope the following examples from our outdoor explorations highlight how we think we can help children become safe. There is also a list of helpful texts in the references section (see Section III).

A good deal of rain can make the ground slippery and in wet conditions trees can be too dangerous to climb. Therefore, it is a good idea to try and help children be self-sufficient by giving them methods by which to test if something is a danger or not. This can be achieved even with very young children, as this diary extract shows:

> "A number of the children wanted to climb onto the felled trees today, but I said they couldn't as it was too slippery. I showed the children my 'one boot test' (made up on the spot!) in which you stand with one foot solidly on the ground (and it is key to emphasise the foot being firmly established) and with the other foot you lift it onto the thing you wish to climb onto e.g. a log. If your boot slips around on the log then that tells you it is not safe to climb onto it today".

The children were able to perform this safety check themselves and they took heed by not climbing. This boot test is very obvious and so easy for children to perform; Figure 1.6 shows three EYFS children performing the 'one boot test' to ascertain whether or not the log is safe to climb on.

Accidents will happen and it is important to let children and adults view this as part of life. Invariably we have diary entries from our outdoor exploring sessions that reflect this:

> "One of the children wasn't listening to me when asked to kneel down next to the pond and despite multiple reminders she ended up accidentally stepping forward into the pond up to her knee. She got very wet, very quickly and immediately started crying, more from the shock I think. She was quickly lifted out of the pond and fortunately the school had spare waterproofs, so she was taken back to class to dry off and get changed and was soon back outside with the group. When she returned I made a point of talking to her about why we must always kneel or sit near the pond. I'm confident that the message finally got across through her experience!"

Figure 1.6 EYFS children performing the 'one boot test' to ascertain whether or not the log is safe to climb on

In this example a number of adults were with the children at the pond and this accident was speedily dealt with and the child learnt a lesson about how to keep safe near water. In fact during a session months later this same child was observed reminding her peers to kneel down when exploring the pond because, as she told them,

> *"the pond is very cold and it's not as nice as having a bath!"*

Just because you have done a site safety check does not mean the site does not need to be regularly considered from a health and safety viewpoint. The following diary entry highlights this:

> *"A group of boys were attempting to take large branches up into the tree they were climbing today. I was concerned that this was potentially an accident waiting to happen as other boys were starting to play on the ground directly beneath the same tree. I called the boys together to ask what they thought the safety issues might be and, not surprisingly, with minimal prompting, they were able to see quite quickly how their activities could have led to injury. I encouraged them to create their own safety boundary by placing logs in a circle around the tree and that they had to ensure that no one was allowed inside this circle whilst someone was placing items up in the tree. They also had to agree*

that only light items would be taken into the tree, which they agreed could weigh no more than a bunch of five small sticks. When the whole group was gathered at the end of the session I asked the boys to explain to the others how they'd kept safe whilst tree climbing today. From observing the boys playing and from their explanation to the group I was convinced that they had understood the important safety issues raised in today's session."

You still need to keep an eye on a situation such as this, as children can forget when caught up in the moment of designing and creating. In this case, through careful questioning a situation of potential danger was not closed down but made safe without destroying the element of challenge. The next time these children came outdoors to explore one of them discussed the conversation he had had about using the log safety boundary and this was noted in a corresponding diary entry:

"I was impressed with the accuracy and confidence with which he described the safety boundary concept, why it was important and how he understood today's weather conditions meant that tree climbing would not be allowed".

So how do you make decisions as to what and what not to allow? Having discussions as we regularly do, will help to inform you; for example, how does one come to make decisions about what is and is not okay to do when exploring outside? From our perspective you have to look at the site from a purely objective and common-sense point of view and if there is something that has the potential to harm, then you must warn the children. Not in a scary emotive way, but in an informative way. And be aware you will have to repeat the information. You also have to be observing and watching the children and space at all times. Particular areas to keep an eye on are things like a pond; sticks/branches (which can be made into something dangerous through careless play); fungi (no touch/taste rules); felled trees or logs (which if you fell off could lead to injury). So the message is, you have to be ever vigilant but that doesn't equate to being ever fussing.

How about things like stinging nettles or brambles at your site? Stinging nettles and thorny brambles are part and parcel of the natural world and they can sometimes be difficult to get rid of without the use of chemicals, which can damage the environment. When children accidentally brush up against a stinging nettle they are generally pretty calm about the whole thing, as we tell them that the feeling won't last long, it can be soothed by a cool wet tissue or a dock leaf (if you have the latter plants on site). We tell them that all the most adventurous explorers get stung once in a while. In our sessions the children generally wear long sleeved tops and trousers, so stings are fairly rare and when they do occur it's usually a minor sting on the hand. Even the youngest children we've taken out to the site usually know what a stinging nettle and dock leaf look like (and we show them if they don't know) – so they know that the stinging nettles are in the site and that they are best avoided. For us it's important for the children to learn that although nettles can leave humans with a temporary, itchy rash, they are a crucial food source for many native insect species, including the caterpillars of tortoiseshell and peacock butterflies. Similarly you cannot stop bees or wasps visiting your site, it would be a near impossible (and pointless) task to try. So we make sure that we know if any child has an allergic reaction to these types of stings and we have first aid training to deal with a sting-related incident should it occur. In our experience children generally know that bees will leave you alone and that wasps are the ones to steer clear of, especially during the summer. So if there are wasps around we make sure the children don't accidentally aggravate them by flapping around, increasing the chance of them being stung. In the past four years of exploring with the children at our Oxfordshire school site we've never had a child being stung by a bee or a wasp (or any other insect come to that) and we have had plenty of these insects present at the site during this period.

Communicating with colleagues, parents/carers

Effective communication with colleagues and parents/carers is critical if your outdoor exploring sessions are to be a success. Some adults will happily go along with the idea of children being outdoors all year round; some will be resistant. Therefore, alongside communication has to be patience; patience in helping those more reticent adults to see the benefits of outdoor exploring. The way to succeed is to ensure that every step of the way there is clarity about what you are doing and why.

As parents ourselves when we give permission for our children to participate in an outdoor session or to take part in a school excursion we rightly assume that the teachers/teaching assistants in attendance are appropriately trained (e.g. in first aid), that we know the place they are visiting is safe, the children have the appropriate clothing/food etc. and that procedures are in place in case of an emergency (whilst recognising that accidents can happen no matter where the children are). Similarly you need to be prepared for adults to have concerns about your outdoor sessions, even if they are taking place at a site that is physically located within your school grounds. We have, for example, been asked by parents if we will be taking a class exploring outdoors on a particular day "*because it's raining and 'X' may get wet*" or "*because it's very chilly today and the children may catch a cold*". Similarly we have seen parents dressing their children in so many layers of clothing that their child can barely move. You therefore have an important role to play in setting expectations and providing clear lines of communication amongst the adults.

The weather and children

Whatever the weather, we need to wear clothing suitable to stay healthy and it is the adult's responsibility to make sure children are appropriately dressed for the weather. Children may say they do not need a coat or hat because they are not cold or hot. Although we want to build up children's self-reliance it can be the case that these children simply cannot be bothered to collect their coat or hat. So we need to make the judgement about what is the suitable clothing for the weather on that day. Suitable clothing will be waterproof trousers and coat in the rain; hat, gloves, scarf and additional layers everywhere, including the feet, when it is particularly cold and a hat and loose clothing on a hot day.

Getting cold is not good for anyone and can render one almost unable to think or act. So in the colder months do check in particular, that children's feet and hands are warm and monitor this throughout a session. If feet do get cold put fresh socks on, which you have blown into (warm air) to restore the circulation. In terms of sunlight it is important to find a balance between covering children up and stopping the critical health enhancing attributes of the sun. Do remember we need light and sunlight all the year round and this is more critical in the winter months when the light is usually not as strong and there is less daylight. Vitamin D regulates the amount of calcium and phosphate in the body and is vital for healthy bones; it is most effectively activated in sunlight. Rickets, a bone deformity disease, is caused by a lack of Vitamin

D and unfortunately in this country rickets is once again on the increase. So everyone needs some exposure to sunlight throughout the year. So for those winter days it is critical to get children outside, and although not always exposed to sunlight they will be exposed to day light. On the sunnier days a hat and loose sleeved top offer protection from the strong UV rays.

Effective communication with parents/carers and supporting adults

We have listed here some of the most important points for you to communicate to parents/carers and supporting adults based on our experience of common concerns and questions. Alongside these we have provided some of our top tips/suggestions on how these may be approached.

What is outdoor exploring and why is the school doing it?

Suggestion: Your school believes that outdoor exploration is an essential component of a child's learning and development and as such, regular sessions will be timetabled to provide opportunities for the children to explore the natural world within a safe setting and with appropriately qualified/experienced adults.

- **TOP TIP:** Outdoor exploration offers a diversity of learning opportunities for children which can build on their learning that is taking place within the classroom. Share examples of your outdoor observations of children's learning and development with their parents/carers. Take time to explain how you build on children's outdoor experiences back in the classroom, whether it is to further develop a particular skill (social and/or academic) or to show how outdoor explorations 'map' onto elements of the National Curriculum/Early Years Framework.
- **TOP TIP:** See an example briefing letter for parents in Section III.

Where you will be going: is your site on school premises or elsewhere?

- **TOP TIP:** If your site is on school premises you could provide opportunities for colleagues/parents/carers to visit the site and/or to volunteer to support your outdoor sessions. If your site is located outside school premises, provide details (including photos and/or videos) of where the site is located and how the children will be safely transported to and from the site.
- **TOP TIP:** You could provide a map of your site showing its size and any particular features of note (e.g. woodland areas). Show the boundaries of your site (fencing, natural hedging) and share how you will ensure children are kept within these boundaries; for example, by conducting regular headcounts of the children and ensuring supporting adults have specific responsibility for monitoring particular areas across your site. This is especially relevant for more densely wooded areas where keeping track of children's movements is likely to be more challenging.
- **TOP TIP:** You could ask for the adults' help in preparing your site; for example, planting new trees, clearing the ground, adding new natural resource features, such as logs and hay bales.

Which members of staff/adult helpers will be accompanying the children?

- **TOP TIP:** Provide details of the teacher and teaching assistants/other adult helpers who will be attending outdoor exploring sessions along with the ratio of adults to children.
- **TOP TIP:** It is great if you can get parents/carers to help with your outdoor sessions as it provides first-hand opportunities for them to see the children exploring. To avoid children clinging to their parent(s)/carer during a session (especially younger children) and to help parents/carers overcome their natural tendency to monitor their own child's activity we recommend parents/carers are invited to volunteer for sessions when their own child/family member is not in the group.

What training do staff have?

- **TOP TIP:** Share adults' previous experience working with children outdoors, for example, leading/assisting with brownies, cubs and scout groups. Provide details of relevant qualifications held by the teacher/teaching assistant/other adult helpers. These will typically include first aid qualifications, food hygiene certification or other relevant training certificates and/or experience.

How will the children be kept safe?

- **TOP TIP:** Ensure that all supporting adults on-site are DBS (or equivalent) checked and share this information with parents/carers.
- **TOP TIP:** Whoever is leading the session should be made aware by the school of any relevant pre-existing medical conditions and/or medication needs that children may have that are relevant to them being outdoors.
- **TOP TIP:** Share details of the first aid kit that you always have on-site. This could be done by taking a photo of your first aid kit with items particularly relevant to working outdoors clearly indicated (e.g. emergency blanket).
- **TOP TIP:** Share your outdoor explorers' rules and how you will explain and reinforce these to the children. The consequences of breaking a rule could also be included, for example, accompanying a child off site for a period of time or returning the child to class.
- **TOP TIP:** Share your methods for allowing the children freedom to explore your site. For example, explain your explorer rules and how children are encouraged to see how these may be affected by local weather conditions on the day of your session.
- **TOP TIP:** Give examples of how children have demonstrated their own methods for risk assessment. For example, in wet weather you might ask your children at the start of a session what they may need to watch out for when exploring today. With children as young as three and four you are likely to get a response along the lines of *"we need to be careful of the slippery ground and be extra careful if we are climbing onto the logs today"*. Show how you encourage children to be aware of the local site conditions and/or weather and how you encourage them to make relationships between those conditions/weather and their choice of exploratory activities for that session.
- **TOP TIP:** Share how you delegate responsibility for different areas across your site to individual adults ensuring site coverage; in this way no matter where the children explore there is always an adult available nearby.
- **TOP TIP:** Make sure you have an appropriately loud and distinctive signal that you give

out to let your children know that they must immediately stop what they are doing and meet with you at a pre-determined place in your site. Shaking a tambourine might work well for a relatively small site with little background noise; sounding a loud horn, like an old bicycle horn, will be more effective for a larger site and/or where there is more background noise, such as a road.

Will you go out even when the weather is wet, very cold or very hot?

- **TOP TIP:** Explain that for learning outdoors to have a real impact on children it has to be regular, expected, and take place over a long period of time. So you will be going out to explore, whatever the weather, as this will ensure the learning is embedded. This is also an ideal opportunity to reinforce the importance of children wearing clothing appropriate for the weather.
- **TOP TIP:** There may however, be situations when the weather is particularly bad, or predicted to be, so that you have to postpone a session for health and safety reasons; for example, storm-force winds or a lightning storm. Let parents/carers know your likely exceptions to your whatever the weather ethos.

How long does each outdoor session last?

- **TOP TIP:** Share details of the average duration of sessions so that parents/carers know how long their children will be outdoors each time. From our experience, as long as the children and supporting adults have the appropriate clothing, a suggested minimum period for an outdoor session would be one hour. However, how long you stay out will, of course, depend on a number of factors, including the age of children in your group; the local weather conditions; school timetabling restrictions; transport arrangements and so on.

What toilet facilities are available at your site?

- This is an important area to consider, especially if children are exploring in a site beyond the school premises or if you are taking a young group of children out to your site who may just be learning to use the toilet.
- **TOP TIP:** Ensure all children (and adults!) go to the toilet immediately before you depart for your site. Invariably however, there is always a situation in which someone needs to use the toilet when you are outdoors. If you are using a site within school grounds this can be remedied by an adult accompanying the child/children to use the school's facilities. For more remote sites you will need to communicate to parents/carers how you will deal with this. You might, for example, cut short a session and return en-route to toilet facilities if the situation is more desperate. Or you may feel it is acceptable for a child to be allowed to go to the toilet outdoors (which we refer to as a 'wild wee'), if appropriate privacy and hand-cleaning facilities are available.

Are drinks/snacks provided during an outdoor session?

There are different reasons why you may or may not include a drink/snack break within your outdoor sessions. For example, you may only be running a short session and it might be taking place just after the children have had a drink/snack in class, in which case there is no need for you to provide additional sustenance. Alternatively, the weather may be particularly warm or cold, in which case a drink/snack will be important to keep the children hydrated, warm and/or cool. If you are going to provide drinks/snacks you need to think how you will ensure appropriate hand/food hygiene and then be prepared to share this information with parents/carers.

- **TOP TIP:** To ensure safe hand/food hygiene you should take clean water, a washing up bowl/bucket, liquid soap (for ease of dispensing) and clean towels to allow the children to wash their hands prior to drinking/eating on site. See Figure 1.7 in which Year 4 children are washing their hands in preparation for a mid-session snack break.
- **TOP TIP:** If parents are supplying the snacks for your outdoor session it is a good idea to request that they provide healthy snacks with minimal packaging to encourage healthy eating and to reduce (accidental) littering of your site.

Figure 1.7 Hand-washing facilities are particularly important when snacks and/or drinks are provided as part of an outdoor exploring session

What procedures are in place in case of an emergency?

- **TOP TIP:** Make it clear that all adults taking part in outdoor sessions are aware of your plans in case of emergency; for example, by knowing the location of the outdoor first aid kit and who the qualified first-aiders on site are.
- **TOP TIP:** Reassure parents/carers that if you are using a site beyond the school premises that all children's emergency contact details are taken out with you, just as you would do if you were taking the children on a normal school excursion.

What safety checks have been done for your site?

- **TOP TIP:** the sort of safety-related information you need to have readily available to share with colleagues and parents/carers includes the following:
  - Details of who conducts the site safety checks, how these are done and how regularly these checks take place (see Figure 1.8 of an outdoor session leader conducting a site safety inspection of a tree).
  - A list of identified on-site hazards and how these are managed to ensure the children's safety.
  - Copies of relevant risk assessments (see Chapter 3 for more details on assessing risk and see Section III for risk assessment templates).
  - School protocol for reviewing your risk assessments and the procedures if/when a new site safety issue is identified.

Figure 1.8 Regular safety inspections of all aspects of an outdoor exploring site are crucial, for example, checking the tree canopy for unstable branches

What will the children be doing in the explorer sessions?

- **TOP TIP:** Children will be exploring, playing, running around, getting wet and muddy as part of your outdoor sessions. Some parents/carers may not see your outdoor sessions as providing much in the way of learning in comparison to indoor classroom teaching. This is an opportunity for you to explain your/your school's vision of outdoor exploration and why you believe it is so important for the children's learning and development.
- **TOP TIP:** Share the basic structure/timings of your sessions. See Section III for an example session outline.
- **TOP TIP:** The children will invariably be engaging in many activities outdoors so make sure you seek parent/carer permission to take photographs and videos to capture these and then share these images, for example, as part of your school newsletters, school website and/or for staff training purposes (see Section III for an example of a permissions letter).
- **TOP TIP:** Not all parents/carers will necessarily have easy access to a computer to view photos/videos of the children exploring outdoors. Make sure you also provide hard copies of photos of the children (with relevant permissions); for example, as a regular part of your class or school newsletter or on a dedicated outdoor exploration noticeboard in school (see Figure 1.9 the EYFS showcasing children's activities as part of their outdoor exploration).
- **TOP TIP:** Explain how your site will be looked after (i.e. site sustainability) and provide information about the roles children will be playing in looking after the site. For example, children will not be allowed to remove any items from the site and entry/exit points to the site might be varied to minimise impact of repeated footfall in the same location. This is a good opportunity to demonstrate how you are teaching the children about caring for the environment.

Figure 1.9 A classroom display is an effective way to showcase the activities children engage in through outdoor exploration

What clothing will be needed?

Appropriate clothing for outdoor exploration is incredibly important. Children (and adults) who do not have suitable clothing and footwear for the weather and site conditions will invariable have a pretty miserable experience. Above all else you do not want this to happen. See Section III for a recommended list of outdoor clothing.

- **TOP TIP:** You need to explain what you mean by appropriate clothing and why it is so important. You also need to be honest and say that the children are likely to get dirty and perhaps even wet sometimes, so do not send your child into school wearing their best non-school clothing and shoes.
- **TOP TIP:** You should provide a realistic list of the basic clothing/footwear requirements that each child will need. From experience we know that children forget their clothes or they get particularly muddy/wet during a session, so we would advise you to always have spare sets of clothing readily available and in a size appropriate to the age range of your children.
- **TOP TIP:** Be aware that many parents/carers will be on a budget and/or have several children to clothe. Think about how your school might help with this to ensure all children have the opportunity to attend outdoor sessions. For example, parents of older children in the school may be willing to donate items of outdoor clothing that their children have outgrown.

By considering these sorts of questions you will have made an excellent start in preparing yourself, as well as colleagues and parents/carers for your outdoor explorations.

Sharing the highlights

It is important to remember to share highlights of your explorations with parents/carers and colleagues. You can achieve this in a number of ways. For example, you could:

- have a dedicated part of the classroom or school displays sharing photos from your outdoor sessions;
- include a regular slot about your outdoor explorations in your school newsletters;
- send out a monthly email, ideally with photos of the children exploring outdoors, alongside a summary of the sorts of activities they have engaged in;
- invite your head teacher to include your outdoor explorations as part of his/her welcome to parents/carers at the start of each academic year to share why your school believes this is so important for children's development and learning;
- ask your head teacher to write to parents/carers to share details of this exciting learning opportunity for their children and show how, in the UK, outdoor exploring aligns with Early Years Foundation Stage Framework (EYFS) and the National Curriculum (see Section III for a letter template);
- provide opportunities to take parents/carers out to your site so they can see where their children explore (bearing in mind many parents will be working, so after-school/evening as well as weekend opportunities to go to the site are important) and/or invite parents/carers to volunteer in sessions or help with site maintenance.

Chapter 2

Supporting and observing children's outdoor explorations

Figure 2.0 A child's explanation of what he enjoys about exploring outdoors

If you provide children with regular opportunities to explore outdoors then you will probably want to record the impact this is having on their learning and development over time. This chapter therefore focusses on outdoor learning in relation to the following areas: observing children; setting expectations; managing behaviour and conflict; problem-solving; developing resilience; encouraging children to be observant; space and place; getting dirty; and linking to the indoor curriculum. Examples are chosen to show how you can effectively record the different impacts that regular outdoor explorations have upon children's learning and development.

Observing children outdoors

There are some golden rules to observing and recording children's outdoor learning and development:

- it takes practice for your observations to be useful to you;
- you need to know who you want to observe and why;
- more frequent and lengthy observations provide rich and reliable data;
- always write your observations down;
- to note a change in a child you have to be systematic about how you use your observations so that you can establish whether or not a change in behaviour has actually taken place;
- do not ever rely on just one or two observations to make a judgement – you will likely be wrong.

Listening and watching

From a casual observation, children playing sometimes look as if they are simply messing about. You need to listen and watch to really appreciate the learning which does go on when children are engaged in play, as highlighted in the following diary extract:

> *"Three Key Stage 2 boys in today's explorers' session were interested in climbing a tree. One of the boys however, could not reach the initial branch of the tree and so the other two boys decided to assist him. Under supervision from an adult this involved the boys working together to create a flat wooden structure beneath the tree so that the boy who was finding it hard to climb could reach the first branch. Observing this activity, two types of language emerged: mathematical and collaborative."*

The conversation between the boys was about a real situation, so it gave meaning to these children. Mathematical language they used included the following:

> *"put it this to this end"; "no, that is taller"; "that's a bit small"; "that's the tallest tree"; "I know it will balance".*

Physical skills acquisition and practice included tying knots, manoeuvring objects to create a safe platform to stand on, working in a confined space and then safely climbing up and down the tree (climbing down is very different from climbing up and can to some extent require overcoming greater fear, as one may have to look down to climb safely). On an emotional level, two children were trying to ameliorate the anxiety of another child who desperately wanted to climb the tree. Through the adult's observation, it was possible to show that this situation encompassed a complex array of language, physical skills and emotions.

Let children talk about their discoveries

There is always something to discover outdoors and an essential part of outdoor exploring is to let children talk about their discoveries. Looking to the research by Bilton (2012) it is evident that if thought is not given to the importance of quality in dialogues then conversations outside can be highly limited and limiting. You can help by asking questions so children learn about whatever they are observing, maybe even enabling them to use new language in context. In one of our sessions, EYFS-aged children went on mini-beast hunts and by rolling small logs they discovered earthworms, slugs, red and black ants, woodlice, spiders and snails (see Figure 2.1).

These children were given both the opportunity to discuss these discoveries when they saw them but also later when the whole group was brought together at the end of the session. Many of the children were then keen to tell their teacher about what they had been doing in the outdoor session when they later returned to class. The related diary observation entry reads:

> *"I was astonished how much these young children remembered, even the fact that we'd found more than one type of ant and more than one type of snail. Their range of contextual language skills was most impressive".*

Sometimes answering a question with a question can help draw out knowledge that children may well already have. It is all too easy to have the following sort of conversation with a child

Figure 2.1 Rolling over logs to discover the animals living beneath them

outdoors: pointing to a ladybird, child A asks, "*What's this?*"; "*it's a seven-spotted ladybird*" answers the adult. However, this interaction could have taken a completely different form: "*What's this?*" asks child A pointing to a ladybird; "*what do you think it might be?*" answers the adult; "*I'm not sure*" says the child. "*How many legs does it have?*" asks the adult; after counting the child replies "*six*". "*Do you remember the name of animals that have six legs? We talked about these animals last time we were outside*". "*Is it a spider?*" asks the child. "*All spiders have eight legs*" the adult replies "*but a group of animals called insects have six legs. So what you've seen is a type of insect. What colour is it? Can you see anything on its back?*" asks the adult. "*It's red with black spots*" the child replies. "*How many spots?*" asks the adult; the child counts and replies, "*seven*". "*Do you know any insects that are red and have black spots?*" After a little pause, "*is it a ladybird?*" asks the child. "*Yes, it is! You did really well to find that ladybird in amongst all that grass!*" says the adult. Which conversation is more likely to have had a longer-term impact on child A's learning? Which conversation demonstrates more effectively the adult's interest in child A's discovery? If we look at the work of Alexander (2005), Mercer and Littleton (2007) and The Communication Trust (2015), quality conversations which develop oracy and then lead to the support of developing literacy include the following:

- children asking questions;
- the dialogue being about current interests or happenings;
- the conversations often being quite lengthy;
- the adult demonstrating genuine interest in the content of the conversation;
- the learning occurring without direct teaching and not involving the standard teacher/ child interrogatory question/answer dialogue.

So in the example dialogue above the child was not simply told the answer, they were given time to think and consider, the adult was keenly interested and the questions were not about children getting things right but about enabling a child to discover the answer for themselves.

Recording learning outdoors

You should aim to keep some records of your outdoor sessions to enable you to monitor your children's learning and development over time. You can complete a one hour observation of a child and this gives rich data and always surprising information, as we often have an unconscious bias which through long observations can be countered. Another way to collect data is to conduct detailed observations of a small number of children for a fixed period of time during a session over a number of weeks (the length of observation time will depend upon a number of factors, including the duration of your session). This enables you to build up a picture of individual children's learning and development and it can easily be recorded on the spot with no additional paperwork back in class. You could also make photographic or brief video records of parts of your sessions, which can also be shared with parents/carers; for example, taking photos of children's creations as they explore outdoors (see Figure 2.2). Another idea is to carry a notebook with you, or a pro-forma on a clipboard, to note down specific things that happened during a session (e.g. by adopting a 'what; where; how; why; when; who' approach to recording) and/or to record your thoughts about the session (see Section III for an example observation sheet template). This is a useful way in which to systematically record your reflections on how particular sessions went. You could also draw quick sketches to show how children use the site during a session. If you do this each time you are outdoors with your group, you will rapidly collate a rich source of information that shows the different ways in which children explore (see Figure 2.3). When notes and maps are complemented with photos and detailed observations of individual children, this will create a detailed evidence-base for you to be able to demonstrate the impact of outdoor exploration upon learning and development. And remember, you do not have to do all of these things for each session and for every child. Just use what works best for you and your children.

Figure 2.2 An example of children's use of natural materials to create their own works of art

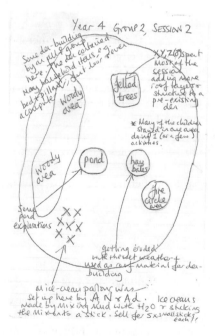

Figure 2.3 A quick sketch map of your site can be a useful way to record the activities undertaken by children during an outdoor session

Whichever way you choose to use record your sessions, collating observations over an extended period of time will provide you with an opportunity to reflect back on the year, to recall the high (and perhaps low!) points, which you can then use to influence your future outdoor session planning. The key however, is to be organised in what you do with your notes/photos/videos once the session is over, so make sure they are always clearly labelled and include reference to the date; group names; number of children & adults and the weather. Make sure your records are stored in a folder (paper or electronic) so that you can readily access them when needed.

Setting expectations and managing behaviour

If children do not behave appropriately it is very hard for them to learn. The crux to good management of behaviour is to be strict but fair; set your expectations for behaviour and revisit these regularly with the group. Children need to know you care about them and that you have boundaries which are consistent whoever you are dealing with. Our tricks of the trade to managing behaviour in outdoor explorer sessions are the following:

- Know the children's names and learn them fast.
- Make sure the children know the rules for your explorer sessions. It is not fair to be told off if you had not been told about that particular rule (see Section III for our list of outdoor explorer rules).
- Aim to have some regular structure to your sessions. For example, using the same entrance to the site; ensuring time to re-cap your outdoor explorer rules at the session start and time to round-off each session at the end. But be flexible! (see Section III for our explorer session structure).
- Expect the unexpected and try to go with the flow as much as possible.
- You do not want confrontation, so try to avoid it. Remember deflection, humour and giving children choices are all ways of ensuring you don't get into a disagreement.
- If a child is told that if they break one of your rules and then go onto break it again, this will result in them being taken back to class, you must be prepared to put that into action. Never say "*if you do that again I will....*", unless you mean it.
- Give children time to explore, find out and know.
- Ask children to find solutions – this empowers them.
- Be aware you may need to make up a quick game or activity to help children if they are stuck with ideas.
- If you are unhappy with a particular behaviour then use your firm, serious voice to show it. Do not shout.
- Be patient, very patient!

Conflict

It is an absolute given that children of any age at some point will get into disagreements, whether they are exploring outdoors or not. Make sure you have a think about how you anticipate these being resolved. To a large extent this will be dictated by how you view children. If you want children to become independent and self -reliant then you would want to encourage them to resolve these issues for themselves wherever possible. Do be reassured even young children will, given time, be able to resolve most issues for themselves, as this diary entry shows:

> *"There was a minor squabble between two of the nursery boys over the see-saw plank of wood during today's session. I decided to intervene as I had just that minute noticed that the plank of wood had two small nails protruding from one edge. I explained to the boys why they should try and share this resource rather than argue over it and when I showed them the nails sticking out, they realised that pulling the piece of wood between them could have resulted in one of them getting hurt. I was able to remove the nails and then I suggested the boys share the piece of wood and work together to use it for their explorations. The next thing I knew they were skipping, literally(!), off into the wooded area carrying the plank of wood between them. Five minutes later I observed them making a new see-saw and playing happily on it for the remainder of the session."*

Resilience

Children need to learn resilience and exploring outdoors whatever the weather (with the right clothing) helps them to gain a sense of achievement and thereby resilience. It's the 'I survived' factor! The inevitability of going outside whatever the weather is part of developing that resilience, as highlighted in the following diary entry:

> *"I think the previous cold, wet sessions were quite a challenge for some of the children who aren't used to going outdoors in all weathers. In this session the weather was better; it started off with some light rain but improved after a short while and the sun eventually came out. It was really interesting to see how this changed the children's expressions – so many happy, smiling faces – it's amazing what a small bit of sunshine and brightness can do to lift the spirit!"*

In this example the children were able to appreciate the nicer weather because they'd previously experienced the more inclement variety. This helps develop resilience and children will learn from these experiences; for example, knowing the importance of layered clothing, waterproofs and appropriate footwear. Being outdoors in all weathers also helps children to understand the weather and further to appreciate the warmth or shade when they return to class!

Problem-solving

There are times when children become frustrated and this can cause demoralisation. Rather than bolster the child with platitudes, think about solving the problem but in a new way. Children may want to do new things outdoors, but they may not have the motor skills, the confidence or the experience. Where they lack confidence or are used to always being helped by an adult, then encourage them with your words, "I know you can do it!" Do not resort to language along the lines of "Your mum/dad would be so proud!" Figures 2.4a-d shows the stages of a child who lacked confidence about jumping down from a log on the ground twenty centimetres high. With an adult's encouragement and scaffolding of help (the adult taking her hands further and further away) the child was able to achieve that jump.

Likewise the following is a diary entry that shows an example of finding solutions by looking at the problem differently. The context was that a child could not reach the first branch of a tree that he was really keen to climb.

Figures 2.4a–d Showing adult support and encouragement for an EYFS child who lacked confidence in jumping from a small log onto the ground

"He kept saying he was quite short for his age (his words) and so couldn't reach up to climb the tree. After spending a few minutes observing him and his friends' attempts to help him, I asked if he thought the problem might be the type of tree he was trying to climb, rather than the problem being his height. I suggested he could look around and perhaps pick another tree to climb, which he did and with a bit of help from his friends, he successfully climbed it. When I went over to speak to him in the tree I felt this was quite a big deal for him, especially as he'd done it without direct help from an adult".

So rather than reinforce a child's issue, in this case their height, observe, don't wade in and then think how to problem solve with them to reach a solution. In this case it was the tree that had the issue not the child!

Chapter 3 covers the essential bits of kit that you should take outdoors with you and we very much emphasise the importance of not providing lots of man-made resources in your outdoor exploring sessions. Instead you should aim to encourage children to make use of the natural resources to hand. This will encourage children to use their imagination to create new games, to engage in role play and to solve problems in novel ways, all of which are important lifelong learning skills. Case study examples showing children making use of natural resources are in Chapters 4, 5 and 6.

Getting dirty is okay – but remember the parents' perspective too. It is important to enable children to be children – to be playful and adventurous (see Figure 2.5). This is equally valuable with regard to building up one's own resilience, as shown through this diary entry:

> *"As soon as the children were able to go off and explore it was obvious that getting muddy was going to be a priority".*

Figure 2.5 Some children will relish the opportunity to get muddy as part of their outdoor explorations

And they did get muddy, as the diary entry continues:

> *"I felt this muddy play was a really powerful experience for the children and for all the adults on site. The children were allowed to do something that for many of them they would almost certainly not have ordinarily been allowed to do".*

On this occasion most of the children were completely covered in mud by the end of the session. It is necessary also to take into consideration the parents' perspective of this activity: not all of them would have been that pleased about dealing with the extra laundry at the end of the day. You should also remember that not all families necessarily have their own washing machines or they might be unable to afford to replace clothing damaged during outdoor sessions. So you will need to show understanding towards parents and keep them informed and explain why you feel a particular activity is worthwhile; in this way you will bring the parents with you. The children in this example were having fun, so explain that fun is about children being immersed in their own world, where there is the physical manifestation of this in terms of smiling and laughter. Why are these things significant? Everyone needs to know how to enjoy themselves because this can release essential chemicals which unlock stress within the body. When these children returned to class the teachers commented that they were full of energy and so much more able to settle to the sedentary work of the classroom. If you believe an outdoor session might be particularly muddy then build in additional time for cleaning up afterwards and if needed, wash dirty clothes at school for families who may not have easy access to laundry facilities. You should also ensure you have sufficient spare clothing for such events and always encourage children to wear their oldest clothing to your sessions (see Chapter 3; Section III for a suggested list of clothing).

Encourage children to be observant and to experiment

Another important role you play in supporting your children's learning and development is to foster their observational skills (see Chapter 6). If you are taking children outdoors year round then even the youngest of children will notice things like the changes in the weather, the appearance (or disappearance) of certain animals, plants and fungi. Engage in regular discussion with your children about what they've seen, heard or touched during a session and we think you will be amazed at the level of detail in which they often respond. Encourage the children to see your site as their own natural laboratory and pose questions that they can try and answer. For example, we have noticed that some children can be fascinated by ice, so if you have an icy outdoor session consider the things you can do to kick start the children's thinking as in the following diary entry:

> *"It was a beautiful sunny, frosty day and several of the children were picking up frosty leaves and touching the ice crystals. I asked them if they thought the ice would be melted by the time our session ended and a couple of the children thought it probably would be, but a few others were less sure. Then one of the children said "if it's sunny the ice will melt" and he picked up a frosty leaf and went over and placed it on top of the log house in the sun. I asked him what he'd done and he replied "now the leaf is in the sun the ice on it will melt". The other children then each picked up a frosty leaf and placed it on top of the log house. The group of children then ran off but I observed them returning every few minutes to see if the ice had melted on their own leaf"* (see Figure 2.6).

This is a good example of children being encouraged to experiment outdoors – and in this example the children were three and four year olds, so there is no minimum age to experimentation!

The fantastic thing about this is that you can then build on this experience back in the classroom to reinforce key concepts, to build confidence and to help children contextualise their learning. In support of this the Year 6 children we worked with stated a number of things that outdoor exploring had helped them with including: *"team work; developing independence and a sense of responsibility"*. Seeing something happen outdoors can also help children make sense of things. Indeed in the ice leaf example there are multiple links to the English Early Years Foundation Stage Framework and National Curriculum at Key Stage 1 and Key Stage 2. One of the Key Stage 2 teachers we work with commented on the value of outdoor exploring for her class:

"The children in Year 2 thoroughly enjoy the freedom of exploring outdoors where they are away from the structure of lessons in the classroom and also relish the opportunity to be outside. It is lovely watching the children who can struggle within normal lessons become so involved with the challenges set and work well within a team. Not only are they applying their indoor learning outside, they are also connecting with nature, using it

Figure 2.6 EYFS children engaged in an ice melting experiment

in a variety of ways e.g. sticks for dens, monster making and climbing apparatus. They speak so positively about these sessions clearly enjoying the outside environment but also absorbed with the element of exploring which is such a natural and interesting activity to do. It is accessible for all abilities and the discussions that occur are invaluable."

Further case study examples of how we have linked outdoor learning to indoor curricula are illustrated in Chapters 4, 5 and 6.

Chapter 3

Setting up your site

Figure 3.0 Children can design their own play equipment if provided with a range of natural materials

In this chapter we will cover the basic information to either help you develop a site from scratch or to sustain an existing site for you to use with your children. In an ideal world of course, every school would have a dedicated area(s) that could be used to support regular outdoor exploration. For example, at one of the schools we've worked at in recent years, Chilton Primary in Oxfordshire, the school makes use of a wild corner of the main playing field area (measuring 39m x 34m) for exclusive use by explorer groups. However, we realise that outdoor space is precious. Recently in the UK for example, there has been increasing pressure on schools to create additional classrooms and other indoor facilities using existing outdoor space to cope with the huge demand for primary school places (Lean, 2014). So, we appreciate that if you do not already have a site established for your outdoor explorations, either within or beyond your school premises, then time may well be of the essence to get one started.

Site basics

The key to an effective and sustainable outdoor site is not about having an all-singing, all-dancing area bursting with native flora and fauna. Rather it is about you, the adults, creating a special place in which children have the freedom to explore outdoors. Tovey (2007) describes this as turning a space into a place; a place has association and meaning for children, where they feel both ownership and belonging. Children then build a strong affinity with the space, i.e. it becomes special. Relph (1976, p.64) used the term 'insideness' to explain how a sense of place is 'above all that of being inside and belonging to your place both as an individual and as a member of a community'. The stronger the association with the 'specialness' of this place, the stronger the children's identity is with it and the stronger their guardianship of it. So ensuring the space becomes a place means children will look after it better. Do not feel a need to create this special place overnight though, let it grow over time. For example the large felled tree in the Chilton school explorers site became the nursery children's dragon and was regularly climbed on and ridden by individuals and groups of children, taking them to both real and imaginary faraway places. Children give such objects live characteristics, which of course need looking after, talking to and feeding with 'chocolate'! (See Chapter 6 for the related case study). In this way children build a strong affinity with the space and place. There is simply no need for man-made additions to this environment. This felled tree is the catalyst for many role play episodes, which will encourage language, problem solving and imaginative skills. Observe these episodes develop over time and this will tell you a great deal about the individual children involved.

This specialness also comes from happenings that occur every day. Children can be amazed by all sorts of things, quite often from experiences that we might take for granted as adults, either because they appear to us to be so commonplace or because we just do not see them as being special. The following diary entry is a good example of this:

> "Once at the site we went straight to the tarpaulin shelter that I'd put up earlier in the morning so that we'd have some shelter from the pouring rain. The children were fascinated by the tarpaulin! Because it was raining so much the rainwater collected on top of the tarpaulin and then started to fall over the edges. "Look! It's a waterfall" said one of the children and then a few of the children gathered around to feel the water as it fell from the edge of the tarpaulin to the ground. The children spent a long time watching and playing with the rainwater. It made me realise that some children may well be fascinated by things that other children (and adults) might perhaps take for granted – we need to be aware of this!" (See Figure 3.1 showing children erecting an outdoor tarpaulin shelter.)

The trick for you is to create an outdoor area that has, or could be adapted to have, the potential to fuel children's natural curiosity whilst simultaneously ensuring the safety of all the children and adults within your group. Interestingly the first nursery school set up in the UK

Figure 3.1 Key Stage 1 children using a tarpaulin to construct a shelter for the group

was on the site of an old rubbish dump (tip) and was called the Open Air Nursery School, as the education happened outside. The tip was turned into an oasis, through the sheer determination and hard work of two women – Rachel and Margaret McMillan (McMillan 1930). Anything is therefore possible.

If you are setting up an outdoor site from scratch it will be important for you to gain the support from colleagues and parents/carers if you are to maintain the momentum necessary to make a success of it. As we have already outlined in Chapter 1, effective, regular communication with colleagues and parents/carers is vital, and in the case of establishing a new programme of outdoor exploration it is especially important to keep these stakeholders informed and to share highlights from your explorations. There are many ways in which you could achieve this and we provided some top tips for sharing information about your site and your children's outdoor learning in Chapter 1.

Site safety

Ensuring the safety of both the children and adults in your group outdoors is of paramount importance. Not surprisingly engaging in outdoor exploration will likely bring with it a number of additional and/or different risks when compared with other activities that you might normally engage in with your children. Chapter 1 discussed risk and challenge, danger and hazards, but it is important to reiterate that the role of the lead adult is to assess risks and to then weigh them up against the benefits associated with the particular activities being undertaken. As parents ourselves we completely understand the expression 'better safe than sorry'. However we also recognise that risk is an important part of growing up and we know that children are increasingly being brought up in societies where risk aversion is becoming the norm (Gill, 2007, Whitebread, Basilio, Kuvalja, & Verma, 2012). Getting the right balance between what is and what is not an acceptable risk is therefore incredibly important. To help you make these decisions, regular risk/benefit assessments of your site and of the exploring activities most commonly undertaken by your children outdoors are essential and indeed will be mandatory for your school anyway. Although we are not fond of additional paperwork these assessments must become a regular feature of your outdoor explorations and they need not necessarily be overly burdensome. The lead adult should regularly assess any potential hazards located within your site or indeed en route to your site, i.e. anything that might cause harm to members of your group (both children and adults). These hazards might include permanent features, for example a pond (see Figure 3.2), and/or ephemeral hazards, such as the presence of ice on the ground. The risk (low/medium/high) that these hazards may cause harm then needs to be assessed.

It is just as important though to consider the benefits of children engaging in outdoor explorations and weigh this up against the hazard/risk components that you have identified. In this way your paperwork becomes focussed on a series of risk–benefit analyses, rather than being exclusively risk assessment based *per se*. Your school is likely to have its own set of pro-

Figure 3.2 Adult supervision is essential when children are exploring a pond

forma for you to use but we have included some examples of risk-assessment forms that we have used (see Section III). It is best to combine this paperwork with regular safety checks of your site, i.e. walking around your site prior to your group's arrival and making note of any changes to known hazards and/or new hazards that may have arisen since your last visit, which you can then alert your group to. We have included an example of a pre-session site safety check form that we use for our weekly sessions (see Section III) and which you could adapt for your own context.

Site location and safety: using a site located outside your school premises

The physical location of your site will have a significant impact on how you plan your outdoor sessions. Things you need to consider will include the time it takes to get to the site; the practicalities of site sustainability and, of course, site maintenance and safety. If your site is located outside your school grounds and you have to travel there either by foot or using transport, then there are some additional things for you to consider. We've highlighted the main ones here:

- The adult: child ratio needed for off-site activities will be higher than for on-site activities.
- The additional cost to the school/parents if transport has to be arranged to get your group to and from your site.
- Travelling time to your site may curtail the time you can actually spend exploring on-site.
- To ensure site safety the lead adult(s) will have to develop a plan to ensure site safety checks are conducted within an appropriate timeframe prior to the sessions taking place. This may mean regularly travelling to the site in advance of an outdoor session to conduct these checks.
- Ensuring a trained first-aider is always present and carries with them a comprehensive first aid kit with additional resources in case of emergency that may be needed if you have to wait for some time before the professional emergency services arrive. These resources might typically include a pop-up shelter; an emergency survival bag; ice packs and burns gel/dressings.
- Arranging insurance and relevant permissions with whoever owns the land that you are using. You should clarify who has responsibility for site maintenance and who to report site safety issues to.
- Your school will require you to carry with you details of any medical issues/medicines and emergency contact details for all members of your group and you should assign a designated, qualified first-aider(s).
- Does your site have mobile phone coverage? If not, you need to consider how you would contact the emergency services/your school in case of emergency. Your school will have a procedure for this – make sure you know what it is.
- Think about where children can use the bathroom and/or wash their hands. This is particularly relevant for hand/food hygiene if your children are going to be eating snacks/having a drink outdoors. You may need to take a bowl, towels and soap with you to your site.

This list may feel a bit daunting, but do bear in mind that most, if not all of the above, are based around standard school procedures, so these are things you are used to having to work with. Certainly do not let it put you off using a site located beyond your school premises because for some of you there may be no other possibilities available.

Site location and safety: using a site located within your school premises

If your site is, or will be, located within your school premises then things like insurance and site maintenance will be taken care of by your school and clearly you will not have the additional responsibility for arranging transport and ensuring the higher adult: child ratio is in place for your sessions. Apart from that, the basics for ensuring a safe site are identical to those for a site located outside school premises. In particular, irrespective of your site's location you should always carry a comprehensive first aid kit with you and be prepared to postpone a session if you deem there to be some form of excessive risk; for example, stormy weather and strong winds that may cause overhanging tree branches to fall and lead to injury.

Really get to know your site

If we had to sum up one thing that you should keep at the forefront of your mind, irrespective of whether you are creating a new site or you already have an established site, it would be – know your site. When you are leading groups of children to your site you need to be confident that you have done the relevant, recent safety checks and that you are aware of any changes that may have taken place within the site since your last visit. You need to be aware of the more obvious hazards, for example a patch of thorny shrub, and be prepared to take appropriate action to minimize risk of injury. This might include pruning the shrub or perhaps removing it altogether, depending on the risk to injury you believe it poses. Similarly if you have woodland or even old logs and felled branches located within your site you may notice the appearance of fungi during certain times of the year, which might lead to illness if ingested; or your site may contain plants/ seeds which could also be harmful if eaten. Although it might now sound as if it is a positive liability to have a site supporting high biodiversity, this is not the case. You do want a site that has at least some flora and fauna – it makes it more interesting and a great learning area for children. One thing you should try and do is attempt to identify as many of the species in your site as you can and the great thing is you do not need to be an expert botanist or zoologist to do this. If you equip yourself with an identification guide relevant to your area (book or an electronic guide) you can work with your children to find out what is living at your site (see Figures 3.3a and 3.3b). There are some excellent, free web resources that we use on a regular basis for identifying fungi, plants, trees and insects in the UK (details of these are provided in Section III). An alternative is to ask a local wildlife group for some free advice and as a school you can then make informed decisions about the need to raise awareness of any potential natural hazards and/or remove certain species from your site which you may deem to pose an unacceptable risk. But do remember that removing everything in your site that has the potential to cause harm may leave you with a rather barren place for your children to explore. At the end of the day it is all about weighing up the risks and benefits and then making an informed decision. It is also worth bearing in mind where most accidents actually happen, i.e. indoors, at home. In the UK, most accidents happen

Figure 3.3a Using fact sheet resources to identify winter wildlife

Figure 3.3b Wildlife identification guidebooks are an excellent way to support children's observation skills

in the living/dining room with the most serious accidents taking place in the kitchen and on the stairs. Every year more than 67,000 children in the UK experience an accident at home in the kitchen; 43,000 of these accidents are in children aged between 0-4 years and a further 58,000 children have accidents on the stairs (RoSPA 2014).

Another advantage of getting to know what is living in your site is that over time you will also notice the many changes that take place outdoors over an extended period of time. Some changes will be quite obvious (e.g. leaf fall in autumn), others are more subtle (e.g. the disappearance of certain insects as the weather cools in autumn and winter) and many of these will, of course, be linked with the changing seasons. Once children have opportunities to regularly visit the same site it is amazing what they will also start to notice and share with others.

Site checklist

We have found that having a site checklist is extremely useful, irrespective of the type and physical location of your site. We have included an example site safety check-list that you can tailor for your own needs in Section III.

Kit checklist

There are a number of pieces of kit that we both view as essential and/or useful to have when you are exploring outdoors with children. You should also think about how you will get these items to the site, as some may be heavy or awkward to carry. We have, for example, used an old shopper trolley to transport heavier and/or more cumbersome items of kit to our site (for example, bottles of water; wildlife guide books; cups and flasks of hot drinks; see Figure 3.4. This has the advantage that children are generally quite keen to assist in pulling the trolley! For sessions where less kit is required we use a rucksack. Bear in mind that you may be putting the rucksack onto wet/damp ground, so you could put your items of kit into a plastic bag before putting them into your rucksack, or instead invest in a heavier-duty waterproof rucksack (see Section III for useful contacts).

We have listed below the kit that we always take out when exploring with children and we have indicated those items which we consider to be essential and others which are just useful to have with you. A copy of this kit list is also available in Section III.

- A list of all participants in your group (children and adults) including any relevant medical information/medicines (essential).
- Comprehensive first aid kit (essential).
- Mobile phone or other reliable method of communication, such as walkie-talkies (essential).
- Tarpaulin (at least 4m x 4m) and a set of bungee cords/small ropes to be able to make a quick shelter (essential).
- Tambourine/whistle/loud horn to gather your group together and/or use to attract attention in case of emergency (essential).
- Spare set of clothes (at least one spare set appropriate to the age range of children in your group – essential if you are working at a remote site).
- Notebook and pencil to make observations (essential).
- Flora/fauna identification guidebooks/downloaded onto your mobile device (useful).

Figure 3.4 A shopper trolley can be a useful resource to transport items to your outdoor site

- Camera (or tablet/smart phone) (useful).
- Penknife – many penknives will be multifunctional and their implements can be useful – e.g. tweezers to remove a splinter; knife blade to cut through rope/string (useful).
- Torch – your children may find natural holes in the ground or in logs and a torch can help them see inside to investigate. A torch may also be useful to attract attention in case of emergency in low light levels (useful).
- If you will be exploring outdoors for extended periods of time or during particularly cold or hot weather, then you should also provide snacks/drinks as appropriate for your group to ensure physical needs of your children (and adults) are being met. If you are using a site located outside your school premises you should think particularly carefully about the amount of snacks/drinks you will need to take with you and as we have already discussed, you will need to think how you will ensure appropriate food/hand hygiene for your group if washroom facilities are not located nearby.

What does a site really need in it to support children's explorations?

We have explored outdoors with children over a number of years in a wide range of sites across the UK, from enclosed areas in a school playing field to woodlands and early years gardens. Things that we have observed early years and primary-aged children engaging in when they are given regular opportunities to explore outdoors include:

- climbing
- hunting for mini-beasts (e.g. insects, spiders and other invertebrates)
- role-playing
- hiding
- stick play
- water play
- mud play
- construction
- making natural art

Case study examples of children engaged in these activities are presented in Chapters 4, 5 and 6.

Key site characteristics to aim for

There are a number of essential components that can help support successful outdoor exploration with early years and primary aged children. We have listed these alongside some additional points for you to consider:

- **Space**: how much space and the type of space you need will depend on a number of factors. For example, the number of children using the site; the age ranges of children and if you have children in your group with special needs you will also need to consider site accessibility. Figure 3.5 shows the importance of having raised areas within your site, such

Figure 3.5 Using raised benches to make an outdoor site accessible for wheelchair users

as benches, to enable wheelchair users to participate in exploring activities. You should also consider the number of times the site will be used each week to ensure site sustainability. For example, regular, heavy footfall across your site may lead to high environmental disturbance, such as the creation of very muddy patches; this might affect the ability of the site to recover from the disturbance. You could therefore think how you might perhaps rotate the site entrance/exit points to minimise this sort of impact and/or periodically fence off smaller areas within the site to allow these patches to recover. If you have a larger site, or a site that is densely wooded, you will also need to think how you will maintain visual contact with your group and how you will gather your group together at the end of your sessions (see Chapter 2).

- **Potential for children to create hiding places**: ideally there might be areas within your site that are more overgrown, or there might be natural resources for children to create their own hiding places (see Figure 3.6). Children need to feel able to get away from the adults, to be trusted to be sensible when they are. To be honest, unless it is very densely wooded, one can still see (or at least hear) children who are moving amongst the bushes.
- **Area(s) for shelter**: it can be useful to have a place within your site where your group can shelter from the weather, perhaps a sudden heavy downpour or for shade on a hot day. This does not mean that your site has to contain lots of trees – if you have a tarpaulin and bungee cords/ropes in your kit bag you can quickly assemble a shelter for your group – see Figure 3.7 (we consider these to be essential pieces of kit – see Section III).

Figure 3.6 Children enjoy opportunities to play hide and seek when exploring outdoors

Figure 3.7 A tarpaulin is a useful piece of equipment to carry with you to enable a temporary shelter to be erected for your group

- **Wild area**: we have already said that your site does not have to be crammed full of wildlife for it to be a great place for children to explore. It is preferable though if you can at least create some wild space within your site as many children across a broad age range actively seek out opportunities to engage with the natural world. This does not have to take up a lot of space or cost a lot of money. For example, bringing some logs into your site or leaving patches of grass to grow wild will create new habitats which will, over quite a short period of time, support a range of wildlife and imaginative play (see Figure 3.8).
- **Access to different natural materials**: although we take out wildlife guides and the odd empty yogurt pot for children to use in pond dipping it is even more fun (and environmentally friendly) to minimise the amount of man-made materials you take out to your site. After all, this is about outdoor exploration, not an extension of normal outdoor playtime with all the plastic toys and resources your children will normally have access to. By minimising the amount of man-made resources you take out with you, you will also be encouraging your children to make use of the natural resources your site has to offer, which may include mud; water; sticks; leaves (see Figure 3.9). This can be extremely powerful in supporting children's problem-solving skills, as well as their imaginative play and ability to make do with the resources to hand (see Chapter 2). In this way children are being encouraged to trust themselves and become reliant on themselves, to be creative and/or to solve problems. These are powerful and necessary skills to have.

Figure 3.8 Logs, sticks and long grass provide opportunities for imaginative play

Figure 3.9 An area for water and mud play is a popular feature of outdoor exploring for some children

- **A special place to gather your group** at the start/end of your sessions. It is useful to have an area within your site that your children know where to gather at the start/end of a session, or indeed in case of emergency. You could, for example, either select a spot within your site that is easily recognisable (e.g. a particularly tall/short tree), or you could create your own meeting space (e.g. a log circle; see Figure 3.10). The latter may be more practical for a site located within your school grounds where you have control over who is accessing the site.

Figure 3.10 A fixed meeting point for your group is an important feature of an outdoor site, for example, by creating a log circle

- **Climbing resources**: some children will readily climb anything given half a chance, whereas others may be less confident or more cautious about engaging in this sort of physical activity. If your site contains lots of trees, some of these may well be suitable for climbing. If, however, your site does not have any tree-climbing options then there are lots of other ways in which you can create natural climbing opportunities. For example, you could purchase one or more felled trees from local building developers, local parks, large businesses or local gardeners who may have trees that are being felled on their land. Alternatively you could buy some large logs or hay bales, which could be arranged in your site to support both the more adventurous as well as less experienced or more cautious climbers (see Figure 3.11). See Section III for sources of felled trees and hay bales in the UK.
- **Clear boundaries to the site**: it is essential that your children know the physical boundaries of your site and you need to ensure that these are clearly and regularly reinforced. In this way the site becomes a special place, special to children and adults alike and where particular rules need to be adhered to, which may not necessarily abound elsewhere. The boundary may be natural (e.g. hedging) or other (e.g. fence); see Figure 3.12,

Figure 3.11 Hay bales provide safe climbing opportunities for both experienced and more cautious climbers

which shows a fence perimeter surrounding a school outdoor site. You should be particularly vigilant in monitoring the perimeter of your area if there are no obvious physical restrictions to stop a member of your group wandering off.

Figure 3.12 Clear, robust site boundaries are important, for example, having a fence around the perimeter of your site

Don't tidy up the site

Children can find inspiration from discovering something has moved or changed within the site, so do not be tempted to tidy up at the end of a session, other than collecting up any materials you may have taken to your site. This is reflected in the following diary entries:

> *"The children really enjoyed playing on the hay bales again today and I think the fact that children in a previous session had moved them to different places made it quite exciting for this group, especially as some of the bales had been made into a walkway leading up to the dragon (otherwise known as the large felled tree)".*

> *"Some of the children explored a wigwam den that had been built by a previous group – this highlights the importance of not tidying up children's exploration at the end of an exploring session as the things children create can be a catalyst for the next group at the site".*

So the site is forever changing and not just seasonally. In this way one group of children's play can inspire another group of children without intending to. Is that not magical? See Figure 3.13a, which shows a pile of logs and an old wooden pallet left lying on the ground from a previous explorer session, which was then transformed into a den by another group of children using the same site a few hours later (Figure 3.13b).

Figures 3.13a and 3.13b Don't be tempted to tidy your site because one group's debris (3.13a) will often be another group's source of inspiration (3.13b)

Final thoughts

If your site does not look like much at first appearance, which may be the case if you have to develop your site entirely from scratch, do not worry. The main thing is that you create, or further develop, an outdoor space that you actually care about and which you are enthusiastic about exploring with your children. If you are successful in achieving this then you will have contributed to sowing the seeds for some wonderfully diverse and rich learning journeys for your children and supporting adults alike, as is illustrated in the following quote from an EYFS teacher we have worked with:

"All the children look forward to their outdoor explorer sessions each week and enjoy returning to nursery to tell the adults about what adventures they have had! Having the opportunity from such a young age to become real explorers of the outside is such a great experience. It encompasses every type of learner and allows them to challenge themselves in ways a classroom environment cannot. The children enjoy the freedom to experiment and work as a team but in a safe, enclosed space. They learn lifelong skills during their sessions about the world around them and how to explore safely while respecting their surroundings and each other. Outdoor learning is a necessity in a child's life to supply them with the knowledge and understanding of the world we live in."

Section II

The second section of this book spans an academic year in a UK primary school where outdoor exploration is a core component of school life. These stories cover our experiences of outdoor exploration with children ranging in age from early years (nursery) through to Key Stage 1 and Key Stage 2 within a relatively small (39m x 34m) piece of semi-wooded land located within the school grounds. The three chapters in this section correspond with academic terms, starting with the autumn–winter term (Chapter 4), running through to the winter–spring term (Chapter 5) and ending with the spring–summer term (Chapter 6). Through these chapters we share real experiences of children and staff co-exploring outside and link to the ideas discussed in Section I. Reading about our experiences we hope you will be able to see the theory being put into practice and also alongside the images, find the ideas more accessible. In this way we anticipate you will be able to transfer these to your own context, whether you are working in a wooded, forested or shrubland area, large or small, within or outside your school grounds, here in the UK or elsewhere in the world. Most of all we hope our case studies will inspire you to get outdoors for the first time or indeed motivate you to continue exploring outdoors with your children.

Frosty winter leaves

Summer acorns

EYFS children exploring outdoors in winter wearing lots of winter layers

Pond dipping fun in the summer

Having fun outdoors in the rain

Chapter 4

Autumn–winter term

(September–December)

Figure 4.0 Key Stage 2 children working together to create a tree den

Setting the scene for autumn–winter term outdoor exploration

Autumn in the Northern Hemisphere, from September through to November, is a period in which there are dramatic changes in the landscape with leaves falling from the trees and daylight hours shortening towards the end of October. At the start of the school term in September children might be wearing shorts and summer dresses, but by the end of the term in December they will most likely be in long trousers, coats and gloves, maybe even wearing thermals. In terms of planning your outdoor exploring sessions at this time of year it is worth remembering that having experienced a long summer break, it can take children more time than usual to return to their school routines. In addition, children will be in a new class, with new teachers, classmates and all the anxiety that might bring. Finally the build-up to the Christmas festivities can be highly disruptive to learning. Adults need to be cognisant of the changes in weather, which can be quite rapid at this time of year. They also need to understand how the weather can impact on children and how their experiences in school might be influencing their children's behaviour outdoors. Be prepared for children to get tired and possibly more emotional as the term progresses. It is also worth remembering that for some children, your outdoor sessions may be some of the only times they get to explore outdoors for any length of time at this time of year. For these children a new outdoor exploring site will be unfamiliar, perhaps even daunting, so you need to be patient as they may be unsure of what to do and what is expected of them. It can therefore be useful to have a selection of ideas up your sleeve to act as icebreaker-type activities, such as taking the children on a 'wellington boot walk' around your site in which you are the leader and the children have to copy what you do (for example, waving your hands in the air) and where you go (an easy way to familiarise children with your site); playing a game of tag or hide and seek (encourages children to visit different parts of the site and keeps them physically active and warm if the weather is cold); setting a challenge of creating works of art using only natural materials (encourages children to observe natural resources around them and to use their imaginations) and so on.

Autumn is a fascinating time of year when some animals might be preparing for hibernation, whilst others may migrate or simply die as the weather turns colder. It is a time when plant growth starts to slow and deciduous trees lose their leaves. Yet it is also a time when many trees/plants produce fruits and berries and when there can be an explosion of fungal growth (do remember the correct terminology- fungi can be the mushrooms we eat, the yeast we use to make leavened bread or the fungi growing outside). Rotting wood, the base of a tree and damp logs are great places to find fungi at this time of year. Children can be fascinated by the variety of shapes and colours of fungi, so do not be frightened of having fungi on your site, but do be cautious. Some fungi are edible but many are not, so the safest rule is never to allow children to touch or eat fungi living at your outdoor site. If you or your children touch any fungi, the following rules must apply: don't put your hands in your mouth, and do thoroughly wash your hands as soon as possible. Have a look at the BBC Nature wildlife site which has a useful section on fungi (see Section III).

Changes in weather can be rapid at this time of year and the temperature can vary quite widely across the autumn/winter term. Table 4.1 shows weekly weather diary entries recorded one year from September to December at an outdoor explorers' site in a primary school in the UK. The range of temperatures recorded during an unseasonably warm autumn demonstrates the change in temperature over this period, from 19 degrees C to 3 degrees C.

As Table 4.1 shows, this time of year can offer changeable weather, which can also impact on how children explore the site. This in turn means although they might have the appropriate clothing on, they may be engaged but are less physically active. This is illustrated in the following diary entry from the autumn–winter term:

> *"I took the decision to end the session 10 minutes earlier than usual as I'd also noticed a few of the children were starting to look a bit cold. I think this is because they weren't running around as much as they usually do, so they weren't generating a lot of heat to keep warm. It's really important to be*

mindful of smaller children cooling down quickly at this time of year if they're not keeping active. Appropriate clothing is essential alongside adults who are keeping a watchful eye on the children's activity levels".

Keeping children moving and active when it's colder is important; they can chill down quickly when inactive. Children do not catch infections outside; they catch them inside, in stuffy over-heated rooms. However, if children get chilled their immune system is compromised and they are likely to catch a cold or similar infection (Johnson and Eccles 2005). Appropriate clothing and making sure adults are monitoring children's activity levels is therefore particularly important in colder weather (see Figure 4.1).

Table 4.1 Showing the range of weather experienced during outdoor exploring sessions throughout an autumn–winter term

Date	Maximum temperature	Weather notes
12th September	19°C	Warm, dry, no breeze *per se*, sun peeking through the clouds.
19th September	16°C	Warm, muggy, overcast (100% cloud cover); damp ground due to overnight/early morning rain.
26th September	18°C	Warm, dry, light breeze, sun peeking through the clouds.
3rd October	18°C	Sunny with lots of cloud, feeling very warm in the sun; damp ground due to morning dew.
10th October	15°C	Warm with a light breeze, some cloud cover.
17th October	15°C	Warm, dry, light breeze, sun peeking through the clouds.
24th October	14°C	Cloudy; light breeze; felt quite warm; damp ground due to rain earlier in the week.
7th November	11°C	Grey, damp, occasional showers; quite windy and cool. Very changeable, one minute grey skies with some blue, then a quick shower, then a rainbow, they back to grey skies and cool wind.
14th November	11°C	Very cloudy; light breeze; some very heavy rain prior to the session and some rainfall during the session; very slippery ground due to heavy rainfall overnight and immediately prior to the session.
28th November	9°C	Very cloudy; very damp ground due to rainfall in the week.
5th December	3°C	Grey, damp ground, feels very cold.

Ideas for getting children (and adults!) active and warmed up during the autumn- winter term that we commonly use include:

- Have a snack break, e.g. a warm drink and a snack. If the weather is inclement, use a tarpaulin to create a quick shelter, which has the added benefit of bringing the children together to share the moment, as illustrated in this diary entry:

    "I decided to have an early snack and hot drink break in today's session (about 30 minutes earlier than normal) to give the children and adults a chance to warm up under the shelter (it

was a good decision to put the tarpaulin up to create a makeshift shelter!) The rain was pouring down by the time we had snacks and it felt really cold. I think the children really enjoyed being huddled together under the tarpaulin – the adults couldn't fit beneath the tarpaulin, so we stood beneath the nearby trees. It was really interesting to see the children chatting and laughing. Because they were all experiencing the wet weather by sitting together under the shelter it felt as if there was a sense that they were all 'in it together', so it felt like a bonding experience".

Figure 4.1 Wearing the right clothing and footwear is an essential component of outdoor sessions. In winter this will usually mean children wearing full waterproofs, hats, gloves and wellington boots

This observation demonstrates how you can get a positive from a negative. It was cold, the children were huddled together under a tarpaulin and the interactions between the children were probably more collegiate than usual.

- Make up a story with accompanying physical actions that the children have to copy. One of the games we play with children to keep them active in colder weather is called the 'polar bear poo' game. In this game the children are asked to imagine that they have just stepped in an enormous pile of polar bear poo. They are told that they must get rid of the smell of poo before the polar bear returns and sniffs them out! To try and remove the imaginary poo from their boots we tell them that they have to shake their legs and jump up and down until we tell them to stop. We then tell them that some poo has accidentally landed on their coats, so they have to shake their hands and arms, run around and move their body to try and get rid of it. All of the children we've played this game with from nursery through to Key Stage 2 have loved the idea of trying to get rid of the pretend poo. They particularly enjoy the final part of the game when we pretend to have spotted the bear and the children then have to run as fast as they can and hide to escape being caught!
- Create an obstacle course or a set of challenges that requires the children to do lots of physical activity.
- Get the children to stamp their feet, do star-jumps, run on the spot to warm up.

Autumn–winter term case studies

The following three case studies are based on our observations of children exploring outdoors during an autumn–winter school term. They highlight the range of activities undertaken and we hope they will provide you with some food for thought for your own outdoor explorations at this time of the year.

Case study 1 [Key Stage 1]: Taking indoor learning outdoors and bringing outdoor learning back into the classroom

There can be a view that learning only occurs inside the classroom and that outside is simply a play space:

> "Frequent lack of attention to the external environment must come from some bizarre assumption that knowledge acquired indoors is superior to that gained outside".
>
> (Bruce, 1987: 55)

One of the reasons children forget learning is because they see no point to it within their lives as it is not applied in practice. We hope through this book that we can demonstrate how, when the inside and outside environments are linked as one, learning can occur in the environment most suited to that aspect of study. The following case study is based on weekly diary entries that track small groups of children from a Year 2 primary class, between the ages of six and seven throughout an autumn–winter term. Note how each group is set a slightly different challenge although the overarching topic stays the same. Through this case study we show how learning takes place outside, how it can be linked to work being studied from the statutory curricula and how the outdoors can become the environment in which indoor learning is effectively applied.

Group 1

"The teacher divided the class into their respective school house groups, so that we would be taking six or seven children per session to explore outdoors. The class topic this term was 'round and round' and so I set this first group the challenge of working together to find as many round objects outdoors as they could within an hour-long session. Each member of the group took it in turns to record the group's findings using a sheet on a clipboard. By exploring the playground, playing field and the school's wooded explorers' site the group found 48 round objects, ranging from pill-box woodlice to the rounded end of a piece of straw. When we were counting up the number of round objects on the group list one of the children noted that the top of my baseball cap had a round piece on top, so the grand total of objects was now 49! Back in class the teacher asked the group what they had found and she was genuinely amazed at the number and range of round objects they had discovered outdoors in such a short space of time."

Group 2

"I had six children exploring with us today, including B, who uses a wheel chair. I set this group the challenge of finding as many round objects as they could within an hour, plus the additional challenge of recording each object's colour, so at the end of the session the children could record their findings in a bar chart. The group worked well together and were very mindful of including B in their discoveries as it was not always easy to push his wheelchair to get access to some areas within the wooded explorer's site because of the damp ground. Whilst exploring one of the children found a walnut still in its shell, so the group worked with B and used his wheelchair to crack the nut open – B was clearly thrilled to have been instrumental in helping the group to crack the nutshell! In total the group found over 50 round objects, including some excellent observations that I had missed, such as round rain drops. When I asked the group what colour we would record the raindrops, they said "see through", so I explained that the scientific word for this was "transparent". When we returned to the classroom the children were particularly keen to show their teacher that they had learnt this new scientific word. Their teacher was also amazed that the children had managed, with a bit of guidance from me, to create a bar chart showing the number of round objects of different colours that they had found."

Group 3

"I set this group the challenge of finding as many different coloured and shaped leaves as they could within an hour long session. I linked this exploring to the class topic of "round and round" by asking them to look for leaves that had round holes or marks on them. I gave them some tree guides to help them identify their leaves and asked them what they thought might have caused the holes in the leaves. They suggested the following: "insects", "bugs eating the leaves", "maybe diseases?" Once they had each collected some leaves with round marks or holes in them I set them the challenge of constructing a table so they could each create a leaf card showing the different shapes and colours of leaves they had found. The children worked together to move a wooden pallet into position as a table and they rolled small logs into place as chairs. I gave each of them a piece of white card and they were each tasked with using a glue stick to attach as many different leaves with round holes in onto

their card as possible. I encouraged them to use their leaf card to show the diversity of colour and shapes of leaves they'd collected. I showed the group how to use my tree guides to work out what trees or shrubs the leaves had fallen from, in this case, ivy, oak, field maple, sycamore, hazel, common ash and horse chestnut. When the children returned to class they were really keen to show their classmate their leaf cards and to point out the round marks and holes in the leaves."

Group 4

"I set this group the challenge of finding as many round objects in an hour long session, but to also collect some round objects they could take indoors on a white tray that I had provided them with. It was quite warm today and I think the children were feeling tired at the end of a busy week. The group worked well together, although two of the children had to be reminded that were we being science explorers today* and that this wasn't playtime. The group recorded over 40 round objects and 22 round objects were able to fit into the white tray, including a tennis ball, a Frisbee, a leaf with round holes in it (which I think the children had remembered from seeing the work from last week's group) and a mini traffic cone."

* Children are used to playing about outside and so it can be necessary sometimes to remind children that this type of outdoor exploring activity requires focused learning and a clear explanation from you as to what they will hopefully gain from the activity. Otherwise some children by virtue of being outdoors simply revert to learned playground behaviour, which may lead to them just messing about.

Group 5

"Today I set this group the new challenge to find as many different round objects as they could and to measure the diameter of each object with a standard class ruler (see Figure 4.2a). They were then asked to record whether the round object was less than five centimetres in diameter between six and 20 centimetres in diameter or over 20 centimetres in diameter. In talking to the children I discovered this was the first time that they'd heard of the word diameter and none of them knew what it was or how to measure it. I spent a few minutes talking to them about what this mathematical term meant and how you measured it. As usual the children were free to explore where they wanted outdoors, as long as they worked together as a team to find and record their observations. One of the round objects they found was a football and we spent a bit of time discussing how the children should record its shape (sphere) and how they could at least estimate the ball's diameter. At the end of the session I asked the children to indicate which diameter size category of round objects they thought would have the most items they'd found in it. They all said they thought it would be the category in which the object diameter was less than 5cm and they were indeed right, which made them very happy explorers" (see Figure 4.2b).

Whole class (all groups):

"I had the whole class out with me today (30 children), along with their teacher and classroom teaching assistants. I set the class the challenge of working in their school house groups to create some monster art (as we were in the run-up to Halloween) using only natural materials (e.g. leaves, sticks, and so on) and to incorporate as many round objects into their artwork as possible. The children were free to create their group's artwork in any area of the school's outdoor space. I walked around

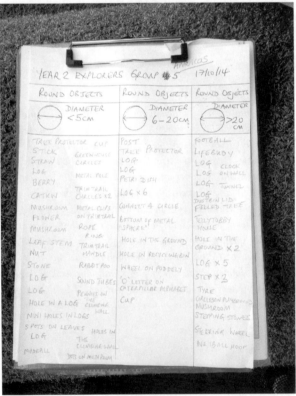

Figures 4.2a and 4.2b Applying skills and knowledge learnt in the classroom in an outdoor setting:
Key Stage 1 children exploring the diameter of round objects found outdoors
(4.2a). The results of their outdoor measurements are then collated for use
back in class (4.2b)

observing the children creating their artwork and with the teacher and teaching assistants we reminded the children to incorporate round objects. When the session time was up I asked the children to walk around and look at other group's artwork before gathering the class together on the playing field. Having walked around all the artwork myself (and in consultation with the class teacher) we awarded first prize to the Americas team, as their artwork was a great monster design and the group had used the most round objects. Each member of this group received two stickers for their class reward chart. I spoke to the teacher on the way back to class and she said how much the children had learnt through outdoor exploring on a regular basis. She talked about how they were learning to share, problem solve and were clearly able to apply outdoor learning back in class and vice versa."

These diary entries show that over the course of six, one-hour sessions a huge amount of learning has occurred. Children were introduced to new language and were able to apply this in context outdoors during their explorations. For example, using words like: diameter, circular, round, oval, segment, width, breadth, distance, sphere, spherical, equal. The children had a purpose to the work they were doing. They were attempting to find "as many round objects as they could" and were in competition with other groups to find the most. The latter element of friendly peer competition helps to create not only an excitement to the work but also can help motivate some children. They had to use their skills of observation (noted in Chapter 2) and apply their number knowledge learnt in class through the National Curriculum ("apply arithmetic fluently to problems, understand and use measures, make estimates and sense check their work, collecting, presenting and analysing data, apply their mathematics"). The children also needed to work together and help each other. Through linking their outdoor explorations with the class topic of 'round and round' a number of simple and adapted activities were invented:

- largest number of round objects
- colour of the observed round objects
- creating a bar chart from round object data
- collating round objects into groups: less than 5 cm in diameter; 6-20cm diameter; over 20cm in diameter
- creating pictures of leaves with round marks and holes in them
- creating an image using only natural objects and incorporating as many round objects as possible
- measuring objects using the correct tools and using mathematical terminology

Every child was out for a one-hour session plus the one hour whole class session and yet within that short space of time the children had clearly learnt a great deal and could apply their learning from the classroom in this setting and *vice versa*.

Case study 2 [EYFS]: Using natural materials (hay bales) to support outdoor exploration and to build children's confidence

Sometimes outdoor explorations and learning will be more adult led and inspired (as in case study 1) compared with other learning. Sometimes the environment in which learning takes place will inspire children and will do so in differing ways, as long as children are given the time, space and opportunity to explore. The following case study tracks some of the experiences children had using 15 hay bales which had been purchased by the school for their outdoor exploring site. It shows how, despite the hay bales decomposing over time, this natural resource offered a multitude of opportunities for children's explorations and physical development. It is also relevant here to look at the theory of Gibson (1979) the ecological psychologist who was concerned with the ecological approach to visual perception. He coined the phrase 'affordance' and argued that objects not only have characteristics in terms of shape, size and so on, but that those characteristics afford behaviour or action from us. When we look at an object we will determine what we feel we can do with it, on it, and so on. A door handle offers the opportunity to be turned, a step to be walked up. So the hay bales are a food source for animals but in an outdoor environment with children they can afford all manner of exploring opportunities.

The case study here is based on autumn–winter term weekly diary entries relating to two groups of up to 12 nursery-aged children who were each taken outside for a minimum of one hour every other week to the school's outdoor exploring site. Some of these children were already familiar with the site having been visiting it regularly since the Easter holidays earlier in the year. Other children within the groups were new to the school and had not previously visited the site.

Group 1

"Today there were new hay bales for the children to explore and these proved to be very popular! Most of the children in this group were happy to climb onto the stacked (higher) bales but one or two children were more apprehensive, but they still played on the lower bales when given encouragement by the adults."

Group 2

"Only four of the girls in today's group were climbing on the hay bales and to start with only one of them was confident enough to jump down from the two stacked bales without asking for an adult's help. I encouraged the other girls to have go at walking across the bales and they quite quickly got the hang of it. You need to acknowledge children's fears but then encourage them, gently, to tackle these challenges independently wherever possible. I see this element of challenge and confidence building as being a really important part of taking children outdoors to explore on a regular basis."

Group 1

"The children in this group really enjoyed playing on the hay bales again today and I think the fact that the bales had been moved to different places in the site made it quite exciting for them. A previous group of older children had moved the bales into a new arrangement and this really inspired the children."

This diary entry specifically links to the ideas explored in Chapter 3 about not tidying up the site after each group.

Group 2

"One of the children was quite nervous today about climbing on the hay bales and always wanted help. I said she was definitely able to do it herself if she tried and that I would be there alongside

her to make sure she was safe all the time. I kept encouraging her to give it a go herself and eventually she walked along a layer of single bales by herself. I think maybe she's not used to physically challenging herself or to having to try and do things independently?"

This diary entry provides an example of how important it is to be patient and being clear about the developmental needs of children. All children, regardless of their gender, must become physically able. See the diary entry for the next Group 2 session to see how this particular child developed in confidence from one outdoor exploring session to the next.

Group 1

"Very few (two, maybe three) children climbed on the hay bales in today's session. The bales are already looking worse for wear after the heavy rains this week! The children today seemed very happy to occupy themselves in mixtures of solo and small group play and exploration."

Group 2

"In her last session this particular child had been quite nervous about climbing on the hay bales. In today's session without any adult encouragement or prompting she was so much more confident and independent and she happily climbed onto the bales and enjoyed jumping down from them. What a difference from the last time she was outdoors!"

This shows the power of encouragement and patience as reflected upon in Chapter 1.

Group 1

"One or two girls climbed onto the hay bales today, one of whom is still very nervous about being on the bales despite the fact that they have really squashed down and are rotting away with all the recent wet weather. I encouraged her to jump down from one of the hay bales saying that I would be right next to her; her face lit up when she did this all by herself. This is a child who really seems to lack in confidence, so I will definitely help her to work on this in subsequent outdoor sessions when the opportunities arise."

This is an example of those detailed moments of observation and reflection as discussed in Chapter 2 and to remember and support children in their development over time. Once again this highlights the importance of these types of outdoor exploring sessions being a regular, expected component of children's time at school.

Group 2

"Most, if not all the children played on the hay bales today. It was so good to see how many of them have grown in confidence in climbing onto the bales over the past few weeks; the majority of the children now readily climb onto and jump from the hay bales (and logs) as part of their outdoor explorations (see Figure 4.3). What a difference from when they first started coming outdoors at the start of term when many of them wouldn't climb onto the hay bales without a lot of adult help and encouragement."

Hay bales are a very cheap but versatile resource which can afford so many opportunities to children as shown in these diary entries. Details of where to source natural resources like this are given in Section III.

Figure 4.3 Jumping for joy!

Case study 3 [Key Stage 2]: Outdoor exploration as a catalyst for diverse role-play

It is easy to miss learning, as it can seem so short lived or fleeting, but the following examples taken from field diary observations of children in Year 4 show how much learning can take place outside through different types of role play over subsequent weeks.

Group 1

> *"A small group engaged in role play by constructing a pretend fire and sat around this fire cooking some imaginary marshmallows"* (see Figure 4.4).

This is an example of children working together, having the imagination to create a symbolic fire and pretending to cook and eat marshmallows. Children need to engage in symbolic play for many reasons (Moyles 2015, Rogers & Evans 2008, Wood 2013). For example, they need to understand that an object can be used to represent something; in this example, leaves poked onto the ends of sticks represented marshmallows. This representation of one thing for another is an important learning milestone. It enables children to make the link between the spoken and written word – the written word representing the spoken word. Symbolic play also encourages children to use their imagination which ultimately, when adults, will enable then to be good designers, writers, inventors and so on.

Figure 4.4 Using natural materials to support role play, in this case, the creation of a pretend fire, which the children are using for cooking their imaginary marshmallows

Group 2

> *"Two children in today's group had used a pre-existing den structure to create their own doctor's surgery. They invited me to visit their surgery, so I pretended to be a patient with an injured leg, which they found very funny. We sat and chatted for a while about what types of treatment they could provide for me, ranging from them giving me a pretend bandage to them finding me a suitable (long, straight) walking stick. Without warning the children then said that the surgery had turned into a hiding place from some bears who were roaming around the site and they started to laugh and shout at the bears (the rest of the group) as they ran past the den. Upon hearing all the noise several more children huddled around the den and took it in turns to try and attract the attention of the remaining children in the group. As it was getting quite cramped I decided to leave the den and let the children continue with their noisy role play!"*

This is a very interesting diary entry – it could be that the children didn't want the adult participating in the doctor's role play anymore, so they created the bears to kindly get her to move away from their den. Children are very clever in this way. What it tells us is that the children felt confident to create new play situations and were inventive in how they achieved this.

Group 1

> *"Three children in today's group (two girls, one boy) decided to set up an ice cream shop. They worked together to build a den-like structure from branches and sticks (their shop) and they then used some water from the pond to mix with mud and hay to create their own ice cream (see Figure 4.5). They then balanced bits of this ice cream on sticks (see Figure 4.6) and walked around the site asking other members of the group if they wanted to come to their shop to buy one. They asked me if I'd like to try an ice-cream. I said yes and asked if they had any mint-choc-chip flavour, which they said they did. One of the girls then stuck a short twig into my ice-cream, which she said was a chocolate flake! I pretended to eat the ice-cream, which then fell off its supporting stick, much to the amusement of the ice cream shop owners!"*

Interestingly, this same group of children continued playing this particular role play over subsequent weeks and the game became more elaborate over time. For example, two weeks after the above diary entry, the ice-cream shop group started charging people for their ice-creams but rather than paying with pretend money, the other children had to pay with sticks, with ice-creams each costing five sticks. As adults I doubt we would have come up with the concept of using stick money – it just shows what children can invent if they are given the freedom, space and regular opportunities to use their imaginations when exploring outdoors.

To ensure we capture this learning we need to observe closely and note down those observations (see Chapter 2 for discussions about observing children outdoors). In this way we are tracking children's development, noting specific needs and helping with those needs and demonstrating the impact of children exploring outside on a regular basis.

Figure 4.5 Key Stage 2 children building an ice-cream parlour as part of an extended outdoor role play scenario

Figure 4.6 An ice-cream created by children mixing together hay, mud and water and balanced on a stick cone

Chapter 5

Winter–spring term
(January–April)

Figure 5.0 EYFS children working together as they explore outdoors

Setting the scene for winter–spring term outdoor exploration

The onset of spring in the Northern Hemisphere is characterised by a steady increase in temperature, lengthening daylight and periods of accelerated growth in the natural world. At this time of year children have now been in their class for a term (or more) so they are familiar with the staff, perhaps made new friends and/or strengthened friendships. They are therefore likely to be more settled than they were in the autumn–winter term. However, do not underestimate the need to re-establish the ground rules and expectations of your outdoor exploring sessions – children forget! The weather at this time of year can be highly variable and it can be particularly cold straight after Christmas when daylight hours are still short. It is only at the beginning of February that it is possible to start noticing a difference in the amount of daylight. For example, at the beginning of February daybreak in the UK is around 7.40am and sunset around 4.50pm, but 20 days later and sunrise is around 7am and sunset is at 5.30pm. This is a significant difference and is particularly noticeable during the week as this is the time children are likely to be travelling back and forth to school.

What is wonderful about spring is the sense of anticipation it brings. What was once dormant over winter is now blossoming. As you move into March many spring bulbs will be emerging and flowering. Make sure if children do not notice these spring events that you point them out to them. Also remember to help children notice as the shoots of plants begin to emerge from the ground and leaves and blossom start to appear on the trees. Children need to be taught to observe these things – not all the children in your setting will have had these learning opportunities. So to ensure all children are keen observers, help them by asking if they have noticed anything different at your site today? Birds, in particular can be fascinating for children to watch and listen to at this time of year. The establishment of breeding territories, finding a mate, nest building, courtship behaviour and song are all aspects of bird life which you can help children to tune into. The Royal Society for the Protection of Birds (RSPB) and the Woodland Trust have websites full of useful, free information (see Section III). Encourage your children to make use of all their senses as they explore. One strategy we use for this is to ask children to sit down quietly and close their eyes to help them focus on all the sounds they can hear (see Figure 5.1). We are amazed by what they can hear and over time some of them are able to differentiate between different species of bird song.

Figure 5.1 A group of EYFS children have been asked to close their eyes to help them focus on all the sounds around them

Many insects and other invertebrates will become more active during this time of year and this is an opportune time to ask children questions to help encourage them to be inquisitive about the world around them. As education researcher Sugata Mitra (Mitra 2015) suggests, ask children big questions: *"Why are insects here?"* or *"Why don't insects fall when it rains on them?"* When you ask this style of question, do not stand there and expect an immediate answer. Just leave the questions floating in the ether and you will be surprised when children in the middle of something else, three weeks later, make a comment about such a question!

If you are lucky enough to have a pond in your site you may notice the appearance of frogspawn as the weather warms up in the spring. This can be a great opportunity for children to witness the entire life cycle of a frog as it happens in nature (see Chapter 6). However it is really important to make sure that your children's enthusiasm does not accidentally damage the frogspawn and the developing tadpoles. We have a rule that the frogspawn must not be touched or prodded by sticks as this can damage the developing eggs. Once the tadpoles have hatched we allow children to gently catch them in large yogurt pot buckets which are white inside and therefore make it easier to see the pond creatures (see Figure 5.2).

Figure 5.2 Recycled yogurt pots with handles are an excellent resource for pond-dipping

We teach the children how to safely return the tadpoles to the pond without damaging them (i.e. do not pour the tadpoles back into the water from a great height). We also do not allow the children to keep the tadpoles in their buckets for long periods of time or in the direct sun and we tell the children why this is important. In this way we are able to turn the excitement of catching and observing tadpoles and frogs into an opportunity for the children to learn how to look after and respect the natural environment. Some children catch onto this pretty quickly, others take more time, so you will have to be patient and not be afraid to curtail frog-related activities if you feel the animals may need a break from your children's attention.

Just as for the autumn–winter term the lead and supporting adults for outdoor sessions need to be cognisant of the sudden changes in weather that can take place this term. As ever, when working outdoors with children, be prepared! As an example of that changeability have a look at our UK weather notes in Table 5.1 from ten outdoor exploring sessions one year from January through to the end of March.

Interestingly you can see from Table 5.1 that the temperature didn't change that much over the 10 weeks (an average of 5.1°C). The range of weather conditions experienced, however, was quite variable, from fog to sunshine, light winds to cold winds and from drizzle to very heavy rain. You cannot completely rely on a weather forecast before setting out for your sessions as weather can change quite quickly. Your pre-session site checks are therefore particularly important to enable you to assess the weather conditions at your site and to ascertain possible impacts this may have upon your session.

Table 5.1 Showing the range of weather experienced during outdoor exploring sessions throughout a winter–spring term

Date	Maximum temperature	Weather notes
10th January	3°C	Clear blue sky; light winds; cold; some frost on the ground (small amounts of ice in the pond); ground very damp due to heavy rains in the days running up to the session.
17th January	2°C	Overcast, grey and damp day; light winds; felt very cold today.
24th January	4°C	Cloudy, grey, light rain; slight winds; cold.
31st January	4°C	Overcast, grey; slight drizzle; cold wind.
7th February	3°C	Light winds and sunny throughout most of the session; feels cold despite the sunshine.
14th February	4°C	Very heavy rain throughout the session; cold wind.
28th February	4°C	Very wet and slippery on the ground today after the week of wet weather; lots of mud!
7th March	8°C	Drizzling at the start of the session, followed by dry, warm sunshine for the remainder of the time.
14th March	11°C	Foggy/misty to start; dry and sunny within 20 minutes of the session starting; the warmest session to date since Christmas.
21st March	8°C	Dry and sunny; cold wind.

Winter–spring case studies

Three case studies follow, based on field notes taken whilst observing children exploring outdoors during the winter–spring term. They illustrate the different ways in which children engaged with outdoor exploration and highlight the diversity of activities that sparked their interest at this time of the year.

Case study 1 [Key Stage 2]: Using a 'top trumps' based approach to develop children's observation and identification skills

The English National Curriculum (2014) for Key Stages 1 and 2 talks about children: "working scientifically" and specifies that this is about the understanding of the nature, processes and methods of science. It suggests children should be: "observing over time; pattern seeking; identifying, classifying and grouping; comparative and fair testing (controlled investigations); and researching using secondary sources. Pupils should seek answers to questions through collecting, analysing and presenting data" (Department for Education, 2015). These skills can be taught in a structured and planned way; for example creating books about "the growth of bulbs", "the development of the frog" and "types of 'fungi'". These skills can also be taught when children are outside as they go about their explorations. Something as simple as bug hunting and identification would encourage all these scientific enquiry behaviours, as the following diary entries illustrate:

> "A small group of Year 4 children asked to make use of my wildlife ID guides today. One of the children noticed that in one of my guide books, points were allocated to different mini-beast discoveries, so from then on when the children decided to go on mini beast hunts and found an animal or plant, they asked me how many points they'd score for their discovery (see Figure 5.3). It became quite competitive but at the same time the children did share their discoveries, showing others what they'd found, how they'd identified it using pictures and photos in the guidebooks and how many points they'd been awarded for each discovery. For example, an earthworm was worth 10 points, whereas finding and identifying an oak tree was worth 50 points, and so on. I described it to them as being a bit like wildlife 'top trumps' in action!"

> "I felt that this Year 4 group were working well in mini teams today. Each group seemed to experience a real sense of achievement when they'd completed their 'top trump' discoveries. I could tell this from the ways in which they wanted to show the adults and their peers what they'd found, in particular, the number of mini-beast 'top trumps' points they'd scored. The children who engaged in this bug hunting were fascinated by the range of invertebrates they'd found and, without any prompting from me, they were very keen to use my ID guides and wildlife books to find out more about these animals".

In contrast the other group of Year 4 children that year were not particularly interested in the wildlife guides and ID books even though the children had been made aware of them and had been told about the wildlife top trumps game which the previous group had enjoyed. The diary entry for this group notes:

> "These children seemed content simply to ask what something was, have a brief conversation about it and then move on to find something else."

Figure 5.3 A 'top-trumps' based approach for scoring wildlife discoveries whilst exploring outdoors

From this it appears that the second group were more interested in finding and identifying wildlife but not researching using secondary sources. Both approaches are part of working scientifically and both are equally valid.

The following diary entry explores how you might use wildlife guides to entice a child into learning something new.

> *"One child in today's group outdoors said she didn't know what to do. This was the second time that this particular child had made a comment like this in an outdoor explorer session. As another child had just asked me if they could borrow one of my ID guides I asked her if she might like to do some wildlife exploring with the other children and she said yes. She took a while to warm up to the wildlife exploring but did appear to be getting stuck in and seemed to particularly enjoy looking for insects and flowers. She joined in with the wildlife top trumps scoring and asked me how many points her various finds were worth. Interestingly she often comes to outdoor explorer sessions without some of the appropriate clothing and often has to borrow items of clothing from her friends. I get the feeling that she rarely explores outdoors and possibly rarely plays outside if the weather is inclement".*

It is useful to have activities which are slightly more controlled, such as the wildlife top trumps game, to help children who perhaps have less familiarity with exploring outdoors. These activities are a great starting point for learning and developing key scientific skills of observation and identification and they can be a fun way for children to work with peers, learn what lives at your site and to encourage them to start observing seasonal changes in flora and fauna.

Case study 2 [Key Stage 2]: Supporting physical and cognitive skills development through den-building activities

Den building is a pursuit which all children regardless of their age are drawn to and may come from an innate desire to always have shelter available. The types and styles of dens that children build outdoors are incredibly variable, ranging from simple constructions that take only minutes to build, through to complex structures that may be built by groups of children over a period of days or weeks. Den building provides opportunities for children to develop a wide range of physical skills, such as lifting branches and balancing materials. It often creates problem-solving scenarios, e.g. how much weight will the den roof hold? Den construction also encourages children to use their imagination by turning their dens into representations of real-life places or into pretend new worlds.

Week after week children were seen to be den-building in the winter–spring term, often adding to dens left by a previous group (see Chapter 3 on the importance of not tidying your site) as illustrated in this collection of diary entries:

> "A group of children added more hay and sticks to the pre-existing den structure on the felled trees today. They made a hole in the roof of the den to enable them to climb in and out. This was a big team effort (boys and girls) with the children working together adding layers of leaves, bark and hay to the pre-existing wooden roof structure. They called it their hotel. I would say that this group of children spent 90% of their time (of a 2.5 hour slot) on this one activity" (see Figure 5.4).

It is also interesting to observe how den-building may enable children to perhaps try and make sense of things that they may have seen or heard about on the news, as shown by the following diary entry:

> "Two girls in today's Key Stage 2 group built a den in the wooded area of the site. When I asked them what they were doing they said that they'd just escaped from a plane crash and had landed on a deserted island. They told me that there were lots of plants near their den that you could eat on their pretend island. They told me they even had a pet dog and pointed to a log in their den. They said it was called 'log dog'".

This is a particularly interesting conversation because it took place around the time when an international flight had reportedly gone missing and was the main news headline for several days.

Another diary entry later in the spring term illustrates how children can have their imaginations fired up and become so curious in something even though it doesn't actually exist. It also caused a group of children to incorporate a rabbit based scenario in their play activities:

Using pictures to focus children's attention on the outdoor explorer rules

EYFS children performing the 'one boot test' to ascertain whether or not the log is safe to climb on

Showing adult support and encouragement for an EYFS child who lacked confidence in jumping from a small log onto the ground

Using fact sheet resources to identify winter wildlife

Wildlife identification guidebooks are an excellent way to support children's observation skills

Using raised benches to make an outdoor site accessible for wheelchair users

Hay bales provide safe climbing opportunities for both experienced and more cautious climbers

Jumping for joy!

Using natural materials to support role play, in this case, the creation of a pretend fire, which the children are using for cooking their imaginary marshmallows

A group of EYFS children have been asked to close their eyes to help them focus on all the sounds around them

Stick play often leads to pretend sword fights

Using logs and string to create a giant bow and arrow

An ingenious cooking pot stand created by EYFS children using sticks and string

EYFS children sitting on their dragon tree

A month-by-month view of an outdoor explorer site at a primary school in Oxfordshire, UK over the course of one academic year

September

October

November

December

January

February

March

April

May

June

July

August

Recording observations is a key skill that children can develop through regular opportunities to explore outdoors

Sharing a pond discovery with EYFS children

Key Stage I children working together to identify a leaf using a tree identification guide

Figure 5.4 Key Stage 2 children engaged in den-building activities which extended over a period of weeks at this particular location

"At the start of the session a group of children started to play in and around the den structure that had been built by another group of children the previous week. Two of the children shouted out that they thought they had found a dead rabbit inside the den. One of the adults went over to the den to investigate, but it turned out that the corpse was actually a pile of rotting hay. I took the opportunity to talk to the children about the importance of not touching something like a dead rabbit (in relation to diseases). The children weren't at all bothered that there might have been a dead rabbit in the den and there weren't any apparent feelings of sadness that this could have been a dead rabbit that they'd found. Rather, there were more expressions of curiosity and questions directed to me as to how the (non-existent) rabbit might have got inside the den".

Death is an inherent part of the natural world. If you find a dead animal in one of your outdoor sessions it is important to provide opportunities for children to explore their emotions as appropriate to the age group, whilst recognising that for some children any experience of death can be frightening.

Case study 3 [EYFS and Key Stage 2]: The versatility of sticks

Playing with sticks and other pieces of wood that are readily available is a common activity when children have the opportunity to explore outdoors. Different activities that such a simple resource can enable range from bow and arrow/sword play activities (see Figure 5.5) through to their use in role play (see home-made fishing rods in Figures 5.6 and 5.7) and in creating a variety of structures (see Figure 5.8).

Figure 5.5 Using logs and string to create a giant bow and arrow

Figure 5.6 An EYFS child using a stick to pick out weeds from a pond

Figure 5.7 Key Stage 2 children using sticks as pretend fishing rods

Figure 5.8 Children using logs and a scarf to build part of their den structure

The following diary extracts serve to highlight the ways in which we have observed children using sticks as part of their outdoor exploration experiences:

"In today's session two of the Year 4 boys spent the entire time playing with sticks, using them to dig the ground and to hit other felled tree branches. About half-way through the morning these boys found a pile of tree bark and spent around 20–25 minutes stripping the bark into smaller pieces, which they referred to as 'roast chicken strips'. They said that the bark looked like roast chicken because it was 'white and stringy'" (see Figure 5.9).

Figure 5.9 Playing with sticks led these boys to the discovery that freshly stripped bark looks like strips of roast chicken!

Some children may use sticks as weapons when you are outdoors and you need to be clear what your ground rules are for this type of activity and share these with adults who are supporting your sessions. There is no link between children using pretend weapons in an outdoor area and going onto use real weapons when they are older. There is evidence, however, that banning an activity simply drives it underground. If you are going to allow sticks to be used as pretend weapons then you will need to have clear rules about their use (see Figure 5.10). In addition this means that children have to be accepting that some people might not like to have a weapon pointed at them. Penny Holland has written a fascinating account of young children's superhero play and her main message is that it is okay (see Chapter 1 for a discussion about gun play).

Figure 5.10 Stick play often leads to pretend sword fights

You may find that allowing stick weapon play creates a conflict with your normal school rules and this is highlighted in the following diary entry:

"Another interesting element of our outdoor explorer sessions is that when the children are in the site they are allowed to play stick fights as long as they adhere to the safe stick play rules, which include not running with sticks, not hitting people with sticks, not pointing sticks at people's faces and so on. However, when the children are engaged in their normal outside playtime (snack and lunch breaks) they are not allowed to play with sticks. It's important that the children see explorers as something special, to be treasured, as the opportunities for such emotional/physical expression aren't necessarily always available to them beyond their time in our outdoor explorer sessions. It's almost as if the children need to see an invisible wall enclosing the site and things that happen in the explorers sessions are special. It's important to me that the children see that they are given different responsibilities in different situations and that with appropriate ground rules and adult supervision that they are trusted to be sensible. From my observations, many of the children relish the new freedom they are given and they accept and adhere to the rules that we set. I also realise that other children will arrive at this moment at different times, so keen observation and patience is required."

It never ceases to amaze us how ingenious children can be when they are exploring outdoors and have to make use of natural materials to solve a particular problem. The following diary entry follows some nursery-aged children as they engage in cooking-related role play and through effective problem-solving they construct a cooking stand using sticks:

"There was more stick play today. Two of the children used sticks to create music by hitting their sticks against logs on the ground (see Figure 5.11). I also observed three boys engaged in some noisy pretend stick fights where their sticks were swords, then guns and finally light-sabres. I had to remind the boys a couple of times not to be too vigorous with their stick play as they were getting quite engrossed; I asked one of the other adults to keep a watchful eye on the boys just to make sure they didn't accidentally end up injuring themselves or another member of the group. For me the most amazing observation I made today was when two of the children started to collect small sticks and put them into a pile. I then watched as they collected longer sticks and tried to push them into the ground above the pile of smaller sticks to make, what looked like to me, a tripod type structure. As they were struggling a bit I went over to ask if I could be of any help. They told me that they weren't able to poke the sticks into the ground because it was too hard. We had a quick chat about why the ground was so hard (because it hadn't rained for a couple of weeks, making the ground dry and compact) and then I helped them to push the longer sticks into the grass and showed them how to tie the longer sticks together with some thin rope that I had in my rucksack. I asked the children what they were going to do with their structure and they told me that they were building a pretend fire (smaller stick pile) and that the longer sticks tied together were going to be used to help with the

Figure 5.11 Using sticks to make music by banging them against logs and trees

cooking. They then went off and found two of the yogurt pots that we used for pond dipping and I stood back and watched as they worked together to balance the pots on the tripod structure above their fire. There was a lot of trial and error and I noticed that they inherently understood the effects of moving the pots too far in one direction or the other – this was complex problem-solving skills at work! Once they'd balanced the pots I went back to find out what they were now cooking. They told me that one of the pots was for cooking pizza, sausages and fish & chips and that the other pot was full of chocolate. They invited me to join them for their meal, so I sat down with them and we pretended to eat. It was wonderful to see them so engaged in their role play and to have designed such a complex structure from sticks was, to me, genius in such young children. This is what outdoor exploring is all about!" (see Figure 5.12).

Figure 5.12 An ingenious cooking pot stand created by EYFS children using sticks and string

Chapter 6

Spring–summer term
(April–July)

Figure 6.0 EYFS children sitting on their dragon tree

Setting the scene for spring–summer term outdoor exploration

In the UK between the start of the spring term and end of the school year in mid to late July the weather can be quite varied, ranging from frosts through to overbearingly hot days. At this time of the year many people are looking forward to the long hours of daylight, with up to 18 hours during the longest day on the 21st June. This particular school term can be quite demanding, with many children involved in summative assessments, which in themselves can be stressful and the outcomes even more so. The summer heat can bring weariness if children find it hard to sleep at night or if they suffer from summer related allergies, such as hay fever, and although children need to be in the sun they will also need the protection of shade when they are exploring outdoors.

In a sense this term is when mother nature shows off what she has been up to during the winter and spring months. There is accelerated leaf growth; more flowers blooming; many more insects visible (bees, butterflies, ants, beetles etc.) and young birds are fledging. If you have a pond at your site, look out for frogspawn in late March/April. Children are generally fascinated by seeing the frog lifecycle in action (see case study below).

It is worth remembering that accelerated plant growth during this term can transform the appearance of your site, making it somewhat unrecognisable from its autumn–winter form (see Figures 6.1a–6.1l). During the summer it can make it more difficult to see all of the children in your group because of the new plant and tree leaf growth. This does though, offer new opportunities for children to play hide and seek or to simply hide away from the adults. If you are in a densely wooded area you need to think how you will keep track of your group whilst giving children the freedom to explore at this time of year. It is particularly important then that your children know how to respond to your signal to re-group so that you can support independent exploration whilst keeping safety at the forefront of your sessions.

Figures 6.1a–6.1l A month-by-month view of an outdoor explorer site at a primary school in Oxfordshire, UK over the course of one academic year

Figure 6.1a September

Figure 6.1b October

Figure 6.1c November

Figure 6.1d December

Figure 6.1e January

Figure 6.1f February

Figure 6.1g March

Figure 6.1h April

Figure 6.1i May

Figure 6.1j June

Figure 6.1k July

Figure 6.1l August

When we think of summer we may naturally think of long, warm days. However, our recording of temperatures and weather conditions over the course of a spring–summer term in the UK show what may seem as some surprising data (see Table 6.1).

Table 6.1 shows that the temperature ranged from 8°C to a maximum of 27°C over a period of 11 weeks. The difference between the lowest and highest recorded temperatures this term was, in fact, greater than the temperature difference recorded for both autumn–winter and winter–spring terms that same year (see Chapter 4, Table 4.1 and Chapter 5, Table 5.1, respectively). During this spring–summer term there were still heavy downpours, as well as more extreme weather in the form of thunderstorms, which can be quite frightening for some children. So it was a surprising mix of weather, when so often the word summer elicits the idea of a consistent weather pattern of blue skies, sunshine and warmth. The lesson here is that the weather is still highly variable at this time of the year and therefore you need to be prepared. From experience though, probably the most notable issues to consider during this term will be the heat and the effects of the sun (see Chapter 1).

Table 6.1 Showing the range of weather experienced during outdoor exploring sessions throughout a spring–summer term

Date	Maximum temperature	Weather notes
25th April	8°C	Very wet and cool; some thunder during the session, lasting less than five minutes.
2nd May	12°C	Dry throughout the session with cool light breeze.
9th May	10°C	Showery throughout with a cool breeze; some heavy downpours during the session.
16th May	23°C	Dry and sunny throughout the session; light cloud cover.
23rd May	15°C	Light rain with a cool breeze; felt quite cool with the breeze.
6th June	23°C	Dry and sunny, very little cloud cover.
13th June	24°C	Very bright, sunny day, light breeze; little cloud cover.
20th June	20°C	Cloudy and humid to start; brightened up towards the end of the session.
27th June	11°C	Cloudy, light breeze; very little sunshine during the session.
4th July	27°C	Very warm and sunny; light breeze.
11th July	22°C	Cloudy but warm with some sunshine; light breeze.

Spring–summer case studies

The following three case studies are based on field diary notes recorded whilst observing children during the spring–summer term. They highlight a number of key areas associated with outdoor exploration, ranging from natural objects acting as a catalyst of the imagination, through to developing children's key observational and identification skills.

Case study 1 [EYFS]: The personification of a natural object

In the site there is a large felled tree, which, through the children's imagination, became a dragon, and remained in this persona for over a year. It is unclear who first personified the tree, but you can see from Figure 6.2 how it lends itself to this character as one end rises to give the sense of a neck. Looking back, it seems inevitable that at some point the tree would be turned into an animate being. When the nursery children first visited the site during the late spring they usually climbed onto the tree, sat with legs astride, or they walked and crawled along it and played beneath it. But a few sessions later, the tree became the dragon and this took the children's play into a strongly imaginative zone.

Figure 6.2 A felled tree whose appearance lent itself to the tree taking on the persona of a dragon for some of the children's outdoor play

The following diary entries are examples of the play we observed children engaging in with their dragon tree. To us it highlights the importance of the natural environment to inspire children's play and demonstrates the amount of physical and cognitive learning which can occur when children are provided with regular, expected opportunities to explore the same outdoor site over an extended period of time.

"*The teaching assistant, who is very knowledgeable about nursery education and development, was clearly comfortable with going into role with the children as they all sat and played on the dragon (see Figure 6.3). The dragon flew and stopped then flew to new places and stopped and all the while the conversation between the children and adults was around this journey. The staff member then suggested the dragon may need feeding, with cakes perhaps being the preferred choice. A conversation ensued around making and feeding the dragon with a huge range of cakes, including lemon drizzle cake, as well as sponge cake, then porridge and coffee. This was followed by a discussion with a group of children about the types of cakes they all liked. One of the children clearly wanted to take the play in her direction and said the dragon was not travelling fast enough. The member of staff realising that the children might need space from her, suggested that maybe it was because she was too heavy and she should now get off the dragon. This was agreed as the reasoning(!) and the children happily continued their imaginative play once the adult had climbed off the dragon*".

This was a clear example of play encouraging conversation, over a period of time, helping to embed all the quality features of oracy (see Chapter 2 for a discussion about the importance of conversation). It also demonstrated how children sometimes want adults in the play and then want them to leave (Bruce 2005). So you need to be sensitive to this and be aware of cues the children may be providing you with when you enter their world of play.

Figure 6.3 Children and adults both engaging in imaginative outdoor play

The following diary entries represent observations over five consecutive weeks and show how the personification of the felled tree developed over time:

"In today's session some of the nursery children were climbing on and off the felled tree with far greater proficiency and confidence than in previous weeks. Anne (adult lead) mentioned to these children that last week's group had decided that the tree was actually a dragon, and this encouraged this new group to give the tree this same status."

"This week the children were continuing to feed the dragon, but this time, rather than using imaginary food, the children collected items and pretended to feed the dragon. From the children's conversations with the adults in their imagination they were feeding the dragon sweets and chocolate, but in actuality they were placing bundles of hay onto the tree" (see Figure 6.4).

Figure 6.4 Children feeding their pretend tree dragon with pieces of hay as part of their outdoor imaginative play

So sometimes children can pretend without any props, other times they need symbolic representation (Wood, 2013).

"During this session some of the children climbed onto the felled tree without adult assistance, which showed us how confident some of them were becoming (see Figure 6.5). As they climbed up onto the tree some of them stood up and slowly walked along the tree trunk and without prompting they held out their arms to help balance themselves as they walked along the trunk."

Figure 6.5 Climbing onto a felled tree without adult assistance for the first time is a huge confidence boost for some children

Being able to steady oneself and balance is a vital physical skill to develop. If children do not do this intuitively it is important to teach this skill. Working with children outdoors provides lots of opportunities to provide these sorts of impromptu learning.

> *"Only two or three children climbed on to the felled tree/dragon this week. Most of the rest of the group were pre-occupied with pond-dipping, stick play and den building. The children playing with the dragon made hair for the dragon using pieces of old, damp hay which they'd collected from the hay bales. They moulded the hair into different shapes and placed it onto their dragon."*

> *"Some of the children in today's group climbed onto the dragon and were keen to make sure that Anne had been looking after and feeding their dragon since they were last at the site. She assured them that she has been feeding the dragon and that she had made sure it was kept well-fed and watered."*

It is interesting to note that some children saw the dragon as male, some as female, but the majority of children perceived it as dragon without a sex, referring to the dragon as 'it'.

Case study 2 [EYFS]: Pond dipping – observing changes in the natural world

The spring and summer months are a good time for learning and developing outdoor observation and identification skills. This case study focusses on the learning that took place through children's natural curiosity about a pond that was located in the school explorers' site. The learning opportunities of close observations of the natural world over an extended period of time cannot be underestimated. From what might seem a simple exercise can come a wealth of learning. Close observation is a crucial skill in terms of the very practical – it keeps one safe, to the fascinating – it might serve as the basis for a career in the arts or sciences, for example. So children need knowledgeable and interested adults about them, who are keen to observe and who know things about what they are looking at or to know where to seek relevant information. Skills both needed and gained through close observation include: i) patience (you have to wait and watch/listen); ii) deferred gratification (you have to be willing to forgo instant reward); iii) the ability to note difference and similarity (when we identify something we then have to learn to know what makes up that animal or plant as opposed to another animal or plant); iv) the ability to identify patterns (often of behaviour, e.g. rabbits live in holes in the ground, pill woodlice curl up into a ball as a defensive behaviour when disturbed), to test out our theories (e.g. do all rabbits live in holes? do all woodlice curl into a ball when disturbed?)

The following diary extracts describe children's fascination with nature as two groups of nursery children explore the same pond over seven consecutive weeks throughout the spring–summer term.

Week 1, Group 1:

> "As this was the group's first visit to the site I took the children over to the pond. Being so young I felt it was particularly important that the children learn how to explore safely around water (the pond is only 20 cm deep at the moment, with a maximum depth of around 40cm in the centre after heavy rainfall). I used a large yogurt pot, with a string handle, to collect some water to show the children the tadpoles that were now living in the pond. It was also a great opportunity to show them some micro-animals that also live in the pond, like water fleas (Daphnia spp.). Some children seemed quite puzzled by the concept of seeing such small animals but when given the opportunity to pond dip themselves, they were very pleased when they'd collected their own Daphnia to look at."

Week 2, Group 2:

> "There was a lot of interest in the pond animals today. In their excitement at trying to catch tadpoles in their yogurt pots some of the children were getting too close to the edge of the pond. The adults were spending a lot of time making sure the children didn't slip on the wet ground near the pond. Despite repeated requests to either sit or kneel down when pond-dipping many of the children seemed to ignore this and there were a few near misses! They were just so thrilled about seeing so many tadpoles, which I can understand, as I still get excited about seeing them. But it does show how careful you need to be when working with children near water. There is always at least one adult stationed near the small pond, so there is always someone with responsibility for keeping the children safe at this site. Allowing children to explore the pond is a really good opportunity to teach them how to behave sensibly near water, but you do soon realise that some children will take longer than others to appreciate the need to take extra care when exploring near water."

Week 3, Group 1:

> *"Several of the children followed me to the pond where we spent around 20 minutes pond dipping. The children were fascinated to watch the tadpoles and to see that they had grown since their last visit to the pond two weeks ago. I used some old yogurt pots (with white interiors to make for easier observations) to collect some pond water to enable the children to see some of the pond inhabitants up close. Luckily I caught several tadpoles (see Figure 6.6); I also reminded them that really small animals live in the pond too, so any water that's collected in the pots always has to be carefully returned to the pond."*

Week 4, Group 2:

> *"To me a major breakthrough occurred this week after only a very few sessions outside with these young children. This time the children did all the pond-dipping themselves using the yogurt pots attached to pieces of string. The children seemed very at ease and confident. They also were much more aware of being careful around the pond, so they remembered to sit down or kneel when they were scooping up water into their pots. They were also generally much more aware of other people around them, so they seemed to be more careful when walking near others next to the pond".*

Figure 6.6 Catching and observing tadpoles as part of outdoor exploration is a source of fascination for both young and older children alike

In the space of only two sessions these children had gained the motor skills, balance and coordination skills to work at the pond, as well as the confidence to engage in the pond explorations without much adult help. They were clearly interested and motivated to explore the pond and this was most certainly helped by having engaged, enthusiastic adults encouraging them every step of the way (Bilton, 2014).

Week 5, Group 1:

> *"The children were ready to go off to explore, with the pond being the main initial destination for most of them today. You definitely need at least two adults with this age group of children when they are all near the pond as it can get quite crowded and in places it can be quite slippery with mud. There was a lot of interest in the pond, especially trying to catch tadpoles. Some of the children used the yogurt pots to collect tadpoles and then named the tadpoles after themselves. It may have perhaps been my imagination but I thought that this personification of the tadpoles led to the children being much more careful with them as they returned the tadpoles to the pond after observing them for a few minutes."*

Week 6, Group 2:

> *"I was able to find some transparent tubs to show the children how some of the tadpoles had developed into small frogs (froglets) since their last visit to the pond, whereas other tadpoles were still only growing their back legs (see Figures 6.7 and 6.8). Although these tubs are great for allowing more children to see a sample of pond water they are a bit too cumbersome for the children to use (you need to lean out to collect a pond sample and then the tub can be tricky to balance in your hands and quite heavy for some of the smaller children, so only the adults collected water in this way today and the children used the usual yogurt pots). The tubs were particularly good though for showing the children how to replace animals back into the pond without causing them damage. Some fantastic language emerged from the children's pond explorations today. These arose through the children's discussions with the adults about the developmental stages of the frogs. Words that the children used included: frogs, frogspawn, froglets and tadpoles. Discussions about the tadpole and frog movements led the children to use words such as: wriggling, wiggling, still, fast, slow, and erratic. This last word was introduced by one of the adults; children can only use new language if introduced to it in the first place. There were also discussions about the tadpole and frog bodies, where children used a variety of words to describe what they had seen: tail, head, gills, limbs, legs, jelly, and there was lots of talk about the different life history stages of the frog developmental cycle. It was really great to see how interested the children were in the things that they had observed today. For me, being able to show the children a frog life cycle in action is a fantastic opportunity to make their learning come alive."*

Over the weeks that followed the children's fascination with the tadpoles and frogs remained high and they were always excited when they caught a tadpole or frog in their yogurt pots. It was also evident that over a relatively short space of time the children had learnt the importance of caring for the animals they found. This is an incredibly important feature of outdoor exploring – children need to understand the impact they have on their site and the animals and plants that live there.

Figure 6.7 Using a transparent tub to collect a sample of pond water for EYFS children to observe

Figure 6.8 Sharing a pond discovery with EYFS children

Case study 3 [Key Stage 1]: Raising children's awareness of what lives in their exploring site through the use of mini 'bio blitz' activities

In an earlier chapter we talked about the importance of getting to know your site (Chapter 3) and from experience we have seen the dramatic changes that can take place within a site in the space of a year (see Figures 6.1a-l). In our work with primary schools we have encouraged children to observe and record changes that take place in their outdoor sites using a 'bio-blitz' approach. A bio-blitz is a type of ecological survey designed to identify as many species living within a specified area over a short period of time. Often a bio-blitz takes place over a 24 hour period, but in our work with children we have used much shorter time periods, ranging from one to two hours depending on the size and age of the group. Very little equipment is needed for a bio-blitz beyond some identification guides (see Section III for a list of useful websites), plastic pots to collect species for identification, magnifying glasses, a thermometer, measuring tape and binoculars (for bird identification). As well as supporting children's observation and identification skills this type of outdoor activity provides children with the opportunity to measure and record key scientific data for your site, such as temperature and the local weather conditions. It also provides a great opportunity for children to learn different sampling techniques, such as using a quadrat or transect tape (see Figure 6.9) to measure a fixed area, to record all the species living within that area at different times of the year.

The following diary entry shows how groups of Year 2 children engaged with bio-blitz type activities:

> "I set each group the challenge of finding and correctly identifying as many different species as possible during the session. This was building on their observation and identification skills developed in previous outdoor sessions. It also complemented their class work where they were studying the changes that take place in the natural world across the seasons. I told the group that what they would be doing was very much like a scientific 'bio-blitz' for the school grounds. The children were very excited. Each group was tasked with using a transect tape measure to work out the size of their chosen sampling site. They worked in their groups to identify as many species as possible within their chosen area during the session. Once a species had been identified (using the guidebooks and ID guides provided, and sometimes with some help from an adult) the children recorded their finds on a sheet (see Figure 6.10). It was great to see the children so engrossed in the activity – it became quite competitive. As the children looked through the guidebooks it was also an opportunity to talk to them about the difference between using common names for animals and plants and their scientific (Latin) names and why the scientific names are important – even if they can be very difficult to pronounce at times! I was really impressed with how many species they were able to correctly identify over the weeks, as well as how much information they'd remembered from previous conversations that we'd had about these animals and plants in earlier sessions. It shows that if children are given regular opportunities to explore outdoors they will build up quite comprehensive knowledge about the species living there. This is a great way to develop children's observation and identification skills, as well as building their knowledge and appreciation of the natural world" (see Figure 6.11).

Tables 6.2 and 6.3 show the results from the Year 2 children's bio-blitz activities during a spring and summer term, which were displayed in the classroom. Copies of these results were also given to each child to take home and share with family and friends.

Figure 6.9 Key Stage 1 children using a transect tape to take measurements outdoors

Figure 6.10 Recording observations is a key skill that children can develop through regular opportunities to explore outdoors

Our work with these children provided opportunities to link their outdoor learning through the bio-blitz approach with core aspects of the National Curriculum. We hope that it will inspire you to think of ways in which you can encourage outdoor learning to naturally feed into your work with your children in class as demonstrated in this account from a Key Stage 1 teacher we have worked with:

"The children thoroughly enjoy the freedom of exploring outdoors where they are away from the structure of lessons in the classroom and also relish the opportunity to be outside. It is lovely watching the children who can struggle within normal lessons become so involved with the challenges set and work well within a team. Not only are they learning about different species but also connecting with nature, using it in a variety of ways e.g. sticks for dens, monster making and climbing apparatus. They speak so positively about these sessions clearly enjoying the outside environment but also absorbed with the element of exploring which is such a natural and interesting activity to do. It is accessible for all abilities and the discussions that occur are invaluable".

Figure 6.11 Key Stage 1 children working together to identify a leaf using a tree identification guide

Table 6.2 The results of a mini bio-blitz conducted by a class of Key Stage 1 children at an outdoor site during a spring term session

Year 2 Explorers: Term 5 [April–May]

Explorer group	Date	Weather	Sampling methods used and locations	What did you find?
1	Week 1	Very wet (constant, heavy rain); windy Temp. = 8 degrees C; 100% cloud cover	Observations only today; used own knowledge and wildlife identification books to find out about the animals and plants we found at the different sites. **Areas sampled**: • Explorer site area: ground level • Playing field • Near the club hut	• Woodlice • Ants • Earthworms • Cowslips • Dogwood • Cherry blossom • Stinging nettle • Bramble • Thistles • Daisy • Dandelion • Tadpoles (no legs) • Wild rose • Pine cone • Fungi • Holly
2	Week 2	Dry, light winds; Temperature = 12 degrees C; 100% cloud cover	Observations were made using different types of sampling equipment: white sampling trays; magnifying glass; collecting bottles; thermometer. The children used their own knowledge and wildlife photo identification books to find out about the animals and plants we found. **Areas sampled**: • Explorer site area: ground level; pond; beneath logs; under the bark of trees • Playing field • Near the club hut	• Snails • Tadpoles (no legs) • Ground beetle • Violet ground beetle • Black ants • Red ants • Earthworms • Millipede • Horse chestnut tree • Earwig • Wild cherry tree • Cowslip • Moss • Stinging nettle • Ladybird • Germander speedwell • Fly • Daisy • Copepods • Slugs • Pill woodlouse • WoodliceRed campion • Fungi • Primrose • Dandelion • Pine cone Pond water temp. = 10 degrees C Burrow temp. = 15 degrees C

Table 6.2 continued

Year 2 Explorers: Term 5 [April–May]

Explorer group	Date	Weather	Sampling methods used and locations	What did you find?
3	Week 3	Temperature varied between 10 & 15 degrees C; gusty cool winds; 50–90% cloud cover; light showers	Observations were made using different types of sampling equipment: white sampling trays; empty (white) yogurt pots; magnifying glass; collecting bottles; thermometer. The children used their own knowledge and wildlife photo identification books to find out about the animals and plants we found. **Areas sampled**: • Explorer site area: ground level; pond; beneath logs; under the bark of trees; up in the canopy • Playing field • Near the club hut	• Tadpoles (still no back legs!) • Pond skater • Daisy • Dandelion • Pond slater • Mosquito larvae • Slugs • Earthworms • Cranefly larva • Stinging nettles • Ground beetle • Black ants • Red ants • Copepods • Woodlice • Wild cherry tree • Silver birch • Cowslip • Fly • Fungi • Thistles • Buttercup • Snail • Bluebell • Millipede • Lime tree • Rabbit • Weevil • Horse chestnut tree • Lemon balm • Elder • Wild rose • Spider • Female chaffinch • Pill woodlice

Table 6.2 continued

Year 2 Explorers: Term 5 [April–May]				
Explorer group	*Date*	*Weather*	*Sampling methods used and locations*	*What did you find?*
4	Week 4	Temperature 20 degrees C (very warm and bright); light winds; 5–10% cloud cover.	Observations were made using different types of sampling equipment: white sampling trays; empty (white) yogurt pots; magnifying glass; collecting bottles; thermometer; white towel on the ground to sample canopy fauna by shaking trees for a fixed period of time (10 seconds) and observing what falls onto the white towel. The children used their own knowledge and wildlife photo identification books to find out about the animals and plants we found. **Areas sampled:** • Explorer site area: ground level; pond; beneath logs; under the bark of trees; up in the canopy • Playing field • Near the club hut	• Tadpoles • Pond skater • Daisy • Dandelion • Slugs • Earthworms • Cranefly larva • Stinging nettles • Black ants • Red ants • Woodlice • Wild cherry tree • Silver birch • Cowslip • Fly • Fungi • Thistles • Buttercup • Snail • Centipede • Weevil • Horse chestnut • Wild cherry tree • Spider • Robin • Water iris • Red Campion • Bumble bee • Red mite • Leaf hopper • Beetle • Small white butterfly caterpillar • Blackbird • Clover • Sticky weed • Greenfly • Silver birch • Ash tree • Germander speedwell • Ladybird • Elder Buzzard • Lichen (on trees) • Grass Pond water temp. = 15 degrees C

Table 6.2 continued

Year 2 Explorers: Term 5 [April–May]				
Explorer group	*Date*	*Weather*	*Sampling methods used and locations*	*What did you find?*
5	Week 5	Light rain; cool breeze; 15 degrees C; 100% cloud cover	Observations were made using different types of sampling equipment: white sampling trays; empty (white) yogurt pots; magnifying glass; collecting bottles; thermometer. The children used their own knowledge and wildlife photo identification books to find out about the animals and plants we found. **Areas sampled**: • Explorer site area: ground level; pond; beneath logs; under the bark of trees; up in the canopy • Playing field • Near the club hut	• Tadpoles • Copepods • *Daphnia* • Daisy • Brambles • Dandelion • Slugs • Earthworms • Stinging nettles • Black ants • Red ants • Woodlice • Wild cherry tree • Silver birch • Ash tree • Sycamore tree • Dog wood • Cowslip • Fungi • Thistles • Buttercup • Snail • Centipede • Wild cherry tree • Spiders • Magpie • Rook • Water iris • Red Campion • Ground beetle • CloverSilver birch • Germander speedwell • Elder • Willow tree • Oak tree • Privet • Rowan tree • Conifer • Swift • Moss • Dock leaf • Buddleia Lichen (on trees) • Grass • Beech tree Pond water temp. = 15 degrees C

Table 6.2 continued

Year 2 Explorers: Term 5 [April–May]

Some of the animals and plants found by Year 2 explorer groups within the school grounds (April–May)*

*Images from the following websites [accessed May 2014]: www.wikipedia.org; www.buglife.org.uk/; www.wildengland.com/wild-animals/small-creatures/insects/moths; www.frog-life-cycle.com/; www.freshwaterhabitats.org.uk/habitats/pond/identifying-creatures-pond/water-slaters/; http://theresagreen.me/tag/sycamore-leaves/; www.plantlife.org.uk/wild_plants/plant_species/cowslip

Table 6.3 The results of a mini bio-blitz conducted by a class of Key Stage 1 children at an outdoor site during a summer term session

Year 2 Explorers: Term 6 [June–July]				
Explorer group	*Date*	*Weather*	*Sampling methods used and locations*	*What did you find?*
1	Week 1	Sunny, light breeze); Temp. = 23 degrees C; 10% cloud cover	Fixed area 'quadrat' sampling: used transect tape and tent pegs to measure out 2m x 2m areas to sample in different locations within the school grounds. **Areas sampled** The group chose 4 areas to sample: 1. Playing field grass near the outdoor year 1 play area; 2. Explorer site area: ground level beneath the trees near the pond; 3. On the hilly area of grass near the 'Tellytubby' house; 4. Grass next to the science area on the playing field. The children noticed that they were finding some of the same animals as when they were last at explorers. They also noticed changes in the plant life – lots of growth on the trees and the grass was getting very tall! Lots of different plants were now also in flower which made it easier to identify them using the plant ID books.	Area 1: • Red ants • Grass • Daisy • Weevil • Spider • White clover • Black ants • Woodlice Area 2: • Woodlice • Red spider • Green spider • Ground beetle • Stinging nettles • Fly • Earthworm Area 3: • Spider • Red ants • Ladybird • Millipede • Black ants • Germander Speedwell • Grass • White clover Area 4: • White clover • Grass • Black ants • Spider • Moss • Ground beetle

Table 6.3 continued

Year 2 Explorers: Term 6 [June–July]				
Explorer group	*Date*	*Weather*	*Sampling methods used and locations*	*What did you find?*
2	Week 2	Sunny, very light breeze); Temp. = 23-26 degrees C; 5% cloud cover	Fixed area 'quadrat' sampling: used transect tape and tent pegs to measure out 2m x 2m areas to sample in different locations within the school grounds. **Areas sampled** The group chose 4 areas to sample, all located within the explorer site: 1. Above the pond area, beneath the trees; 2. Beneath the trees at the far end of the explorer site near the old 'composter' area; 3. Immediately next to the pond; 4. Adjacent to the school gardening area. I asked the group what they thought was different about the explorer site compared with their last visit. They observed and/or commented on the following: • How much the grass has grown; • How many leaves have grown on all the trees; • How dry the ground is compared with their last visit; • Fruits are starting to grow on some of the wild cherry trees; • Different 'bugs' are visible, noticeably butterflies.	Area 1: • Stinging nettles • Elder • Grass • Fly • Black ants • Woodlice Area 2: • Slug • Millipede • Woodlice • Spider • Stinging nettles • Fly Area 3: • Spider • Red ants • Black ants • Red Campion • Meadow's crane bill flowers • Stinging nettles • Grass Area 4: • Elder • Wild cherry tree • Fly • Spider • Millipede • Black ants • Woodlice

Table 6.3 continued

Year 2 Explorers: Term 6 [June–July]

Explorer group	Date	Weather	Sampling methods used and locations	What did you find?
3	Week 3	Sunny, humid); Temp. = 20 degrees C; 45% cloud cover	Fixed area 'quadrat' sampling: used transect tape and tent pegs to measure out 2m x 2m areas to sample in different locations within the school grounds. **Areas sampled** The group chose 3 areas to sample: 1. Explorer site area: beneath the tree canopy near the edge of the site; 2. Explorer site area: next to the felled tree; 3. On the hilly area of grass near the 'Tellytubby' house. I asked the group what they thought was different about the explorer site compared with their last visit. They observed and/or commented on the following: • How much the grass has grown; • How tall many of the plants have grown; • Fruits are starting to grow on some of the wild cherry trees. The group commented on the differences in the animals and plants that were found in the different quadrats. They predicted that an area with more ground cover (e.g. grass) would have more species of bugs than a patch of dry ground beneath a tree. However, their data showed more invertebrates living beneath the trees than in the grassy areas. We talked about the extent to which these data may have been influenced by how carefully each area was sampled!	Area 1: • Earthworm • Woodlice • Springtail • Black ant • Red mite • Moth • Earwig • Snail • Spider (2 different species) Area 2: • Spider (3 different species) • Woodlice • Beetle • Beetle larva • Thistle • Grass (2 different species) Area 3: • Fly • Thistle • White clover • Dandelion • Grass • Daisy • Hoverfly • Beetle • 2 unidentified species of plant

Table 6.3 continued

Year 2 Explorers: Term 6 [June–July]

Explorer group	Date	Weather	Sampling methods used and locations	What did you find?
4	Week 4	Cloudy, quite humid, light breeze); Temp. = 19 degrees C; 95% cloud cover	Fixed area 'quadrat' sampling: used transect tape and tent pegs to measure out 2m x 2m areas to sample in different locations within the school grounds. **Areas sampled** The group chose 3 areas to sample: 1. On the 'mud mound' next to the fence on the playing field; 2. Explorer site area: beneath the tree canopy next to the school's gardening area; 3. Explorer site area: in the wooded area (very dry ground) beneath the trees. I asked the group what they thought was different about the school grounds compared with their last outing at explorers group. They commented on the following: • How much the grass has grown; • More bees and butterflies flying around; • Fruits are starting to grow on some of the wild cherry trees.	<u>Area 1:</u> • Spider • Grass • Stinging nettles • Buttercup • Dandelions • Beetle • Bugle (plant) • Sycamore tree <u>Area 2:</u> • Black ants • Red ants • Ground beetle • Grass • White clover • Earthworm • Moss • Field maple • Leafhopper • Lichen • Spider • Fly • Woodlice <u>Area 3:</u> • Lichen • Black ant • Moss • Wild cherry tree • Elder • Blackthorn • Stinging nettles • Thistle

Table 6.3 continued

Year 2 Explorers: Term 6 [June–July]				
Explorer group	*Date*	*Weather*	*Sampling methods used and locations*	*What did you find?*
5	Week 5	Very sunny and warm; light breeze; Temp. = 27 degrees C; 5% cloud cover	Fixed area 'quadrat' sampling: used transect tape and tent pegs to measure out 2m x 2m areas to sample in different locations within the school grounds. **Areas sampled** The group chose 4 areas to sample: 1. Explorer site area: within the felled tree area; 2. Explorer site area: at the 'mud mound area; 3. On the playing field: near the science area; 4. On the playing field near the mud mound area (dry). I asked the group what they thought was different about the school grounds compared with their last outing at explorers group. They commented on the following: • The warmer weather because of the change in time of year/season from late spring to summer; • More bees and butterflies flying around; • Lots of leaves on the trees and some fruits and seeds developing.	Area 1: • Beetle • Thistle • Stinging nettle • Grass • Spider • Millipede • Moss • Lichen • Butterfly • Woodlice • Fly Area 2: • Black ants • Ground beetle • Grass • Woodlice • Hedge bindweed • White clover • Shield bug • Buttercup • Stinging nettles • Spider • Earthworm • Ash tree Area 3: • Grass • Woodlice • Ground beetle • Back ants • Spider • White clover • andelion • Butterfly • Lichen Area 4: • Grass • Ground beetle • White clover • Dandelion

Table 6.3 continued

Year 2 Explorers: Term 6 [June–July]

Explorer group	Date	Weather	Sampling methods used and locations	What did you find?

Some of the animals and plants found by Year 2 explorer groups within the school grounds (Week 6)*

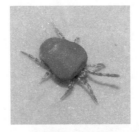

Photo: Male Green Orb-weaver spider (by G. Bradley)   www.uksafari.com

*Images from the following websites [accessed July 2014]: www.wikipedia.org; www.buglife.org.uk/; www.wildengland.com/wild-animals/small-creatures/insects/moths; www.frog-life-cycle.com/; www.freshwaterhabitats.org.uk/habitats/pond/identifying-creatures-pond/water-slaters/; http://theresagreen.me/tag/sycamore-leaves/; www.plantlife.org.uk/wild_plants/plant_species/cowslip; www.treesforlife.org.uk/forest/ecological/mimicry.html; http://en.wikipedia.org/wiki/Trifolium_repens; www.uksafari.com/gorbweaver.htm; www.seasonalwildflowers.com/april/germander-speedwell.html; www.cometpestcontrol.co.uk/ants.php; www.glaucus.org.uk/Pixieland.html; http://blog.38degrees.org.uk/tag/bees/page/2/; www.nhm.ac.uk/nature-online/british-natural-history/urban-tree-survey/results-and-findings/cherry-tree-findings/index.html; www.pocketfarm.co.uk/stinging-nettles/; www.bugbotherer.org.uk/bugbotherer/wildflowers/campion.htm; www.fcps.edu/islandcreekes/ecology/common_black_ground_beetle.htm

Section III

In this section of the book we provide a variety of information, including examples of various pro-forma, and templates which you can use and/or adapt, alongside checklists for equipment, clothing and suggested outdoor explorer rules. This section also includes some links to useful sources of information, resources and references related to outdoor exploring.

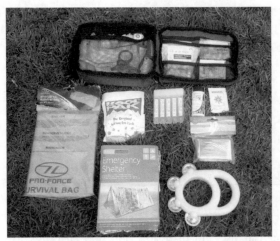

First aid kit and other essential outdoor exploring equipment

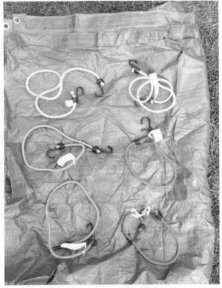

A tarpaulin and bungee cords are a useful addition to have for outdoor exploring to make a quick shelter

A4 wildlife identification sheets in a folder are a useful resource as part of outdoor exploring sessions

Logs, tree stumps and felled trees are excellent natural resources for children to explore outdoors

Hay bales are a cheap natural resource that can provide a range of learning and play opportunities for children

Bibliography

Alexander, R.J. (2005) *Talking to Learn: Oracy revisited*. In C. Conner, (ed.), *Teaching Texts*, pp. 75–93. Nottingham: National College for School Leadership.

Bilton, H. (2010) Outdoor Learning in the Early Years. Management and Innovation. Abingdon: Routledge.

Bilton, H. (2012) The type and frequency of interactions that occur between staff and children outside in Early Years Foundation Stage settings during a fixed playtime period when there are tricycles available. *European Early Childhood Education Research Journal* 20, 3, 403–421. doi: 10.1080/1350293X.2012.704763.

Bilton, H. (2014) *Playing Outside: Activities, ideas and inspiration for the Early Years*. Abingdon: Routledge.

Blurton-Jones, N. (1967) An ethological study of some aspects of social behaviour of children in nursery school, pp. 347–68. In Morris, D. *Primate Ethology*. London: Weidenfeld and Nicolson.

Bruce, T. (1987) *Early Childhood Education*. London: Hodder and Stoughton.

Bruce, T. (2005) *Early Childhood Education (3rd edn)*. London: Hodder and Stoughton.

Dillon, J., Morris, M., O'Donnell, L., Reid, A., Rickinson, M. and Scott, W. (2005) *Engaging and Learning with the Outdoors- The Final Report of the Outdoor Classroom in a Rural Context Action Research Project. Slough: NFER.*

www.nfer.ac.uk/publications/OCR01/OCR01.pdf (accessed 10 June 2015).

Department for Education (2015) *National Curriculum in England: Science Programmes of Study*. London: Gov.Uk. www.gov.uk/government/publications/national-curriculum-in-england-science-programmes-of-study (accessed 15 May 2015).

Gibson, J.J. (1979) *The Ecological Approach to Visual Perception*. Boston, MA: Houghton. Mifflin.

Gill, T. (2007) *No Fear: Growing up in a Risk Averse Society*. London: Calouste Gulbenkian Foundation.

HSE (2015) Health and Safety Executive www.hse.gov.uk/services/education/sensible-leadership/getting-balance-right.htm#sensible (accessed 23 April 2015).

Holland, P. (2003) *We Do Not Play With Guns Here. War, Weapon and Superhero Play in the Early Years*. Maidenhead: Open University Press.

Johnson. C. and Eccles, R. (2005) Acute Cooling of the Feet and the Onset of Common Cold Symptoms. *Family Practice*, 22, 6: 608–613. doi: 10.1093/fampra/cmi072.

Lean, G. (2014) *"Is it game over for school playing fields?" The Telegraph*. www.telegraph.co.uk/sport/other-sports/schoolsports/11092344/Is-it-game-over-for-school-playing-fields.html (accessed 29 December 2014).

McMillan, M. (1930). *The Nursery School*. London: Dent and Sons.

Mercer, N. and Littleton, K. (2007) *Dialogue and the Development of Children's Thinking. A Sociocultural Approach*. Abingdon: Routledge.

Mitra, S. (2015) www.ted.com/speakers/sugata_mitra (accessed 25 May 2015).

Moyles, J. (ed.) (2015) *The Excellence of Play*. Maidenhead: Open University Press.

Muñoz, S-A. (2009) Children in the Outdoors. A Literature Review. Forres, Scotland: Sustainable Development Research Centre. www.educationscotland.gov.uk/images/Children%20in%20the%20outdoors%20literature%20review_tcm4-597028.pdf (accessed 10 June 2015).

Relph, E. (1976) *Place and Placelessness*. London: Pion.

Rogers, S. and Evans, J. (2008) *Inside Role Play in Early Childhood Education. Researching Young Children's Perspectives*. Abingdon: Routledge.

RoSPA (2014) *Accidents to Children*. www.rospa.com/homesafety/adviceandinformation/childsafety/accidents-to-children.aspx#where (accessed 30 December 2014).

Tovey, H. (2007) *Playing Outdoors. Spaces and Places, Risk and Challenge*. Maidenhead: Open University Press.

The Communication Trust. (2015) Importance of communication. Retrieved from: www.thecommunicationtrust.org.uk/about-the-trust/importance-of-communication/ (accessed 23 January 2015).

Waller, T., Sandseter, E., Wyver, S., Arlemalm-Hagser, E., and Maynard. T. (2010) The dynamics of early childhood spaces: opportunities for outdoor play? European Early Childhood Education Research Journal, 18 (4), pp. 437-443.

Whitebread, D., Basilio, M., Kuvalja, M. & Verma, M. (2012) *The Importance o Play: A Report on the Value of Children's Play with a Series of Policy Recommendations*. Brussels, Belgium: Toys Industries for Europe.

Wood, E. and Attfield, J. (2013) *Play, Learning and the Early Childhood Curriculum*. London: Sage.

Forms, templates and checklists

- Example of a primary school site risk assessment
- Example of an outdoor exploring briefing guide for parents
- Example permissions letter to parents
- Examples of outdoor exploring activity risk assessments
- Explorer session clothing
- Example of explorer session structure
- Kit list
- Observation sheet template
- Outdoor explorer rules
- Outdoor exploring pre-session site safety check list template

Example of a primary school site risk assessment[1]

Location:			Name:		Date:	

Description of site:
The Site at XXX School is located in the 'wilderness' area of the school's playing field and is approximately a one minute walk from the main school building. The site is bounded to the rear and one side by the school's perimeter fencing and to the other side and front by newly planted hedging and one metre high fence. The site is secured with a coded padlock. The site is about 60% clearing with a small amount of brambles and with an unfenced pond. There is a range of flora and fauna at the site. The main trees present are wild cherry, ash, beech and silver birch.

Hazard	Harm	People at risk	Probability	Severity	Rating	Measures (new or existing)	Who is responsible?
Low branches	Minor injury	All	3	1	3	Brief children to raise awareness of the hazard Ensure branch levels are incorporated within safety sweep prior to each session	All supporting adults Session leader
Brambles/ sharp flora	Minor injury (cuts/ grazes)	All	3	1	3	Ensure children and all supporting adults wear appropriate clothing and all are briefed of the hazard prior to reaching the site Monitor growth of brambles and cut back if necessary Brief ways of safe movement within the site (reiterate the no running rule) Ensure adults are aware of the trained first aiders within the school building	Session leader
Stings/bites	Minor injury – allergic reaction	All	2	5	10	Ensure children and all supporting adults wear appropriate clothing and all are briefed of the hazard prior to reaching the site All adult and children's medical information (e.g. any known allergies) Avoid areas where concentration of stinging plants (e.g. nettles) is greatest	Session leader All supporting adults

Hazard	Who is affected	Likelihood	Severity	Risk rating	Control measures	Who is responsible
Falling branches	Minor to serious injury	All	1	5	5	Safety sweep of the site prior to the visit to check status of all trees Avoid any areas where there may be reason to suspect falling deadwood/branches Contact the school's tree surgeon to deal with any problem branches	Session leader
Falling into the pond	Minor to serious injury (the pond is not deep but there is a risk of injury should an adult or child fall into the pond)	All	1	5	5	Ensure adults and children are briefed on safe behaviour near to the pond (e.g. kneeling or sitting when near the pond edge) Extra adult vigilance of children when playing near to the pond e.g. designate an adult to supervise the pond area throughout the session Ensure adults are aware of the life-saving facilities available at the site for a pond rescue (a lifebuoy is situated next to the pond)	Session leader
Litter	Minor injury	All	1	2	2	During the safety sweep remove any litter before the session Carefully dispose of any sharp materials (e.g. glass) in the school's sharps box	Session leader
Rabbit holes	Trips and falls – minor injury	All	2	1	2	Ensure all supporting adults and children have appropriate footwear Avoid any areas where there are rabbit holes Brief the children on safe play in areas where there are rabbit holes	Session leader All supporting adults
Uneven surfaces	Trips and falls – minor injury	All	3	1	3	Brief the children on safe movements within the site Ensure all supporting adults and children have appropriate footwear	Session leader All supporting adults

Hazard	Harm	People at risk	Probability	Severity	Rating	Measures (new or existing)	Who is responsible?
Weather	Too cold/wet or too hot – minor to severe	All	1	5	5	Ensure children and all supporting adults wear appropriate clothing Check the weather prior to the session Cancel session if severe weather is expected	Session leader
Dog/cat other animal faeces	Minor illness	All	2	1	2	Check for dog and natural droppings as part of the pre-session safety sweep Remove faeces and dispose of appropriately Avoid areas where there have been droppings (if practicable) Carry gloves, bags and hand sanitizer Ensure children and adults are aware of the importance of hand hygiene and provide hand washing facilities if drinks and snacks are to be provided during the session	Session leader
Fall from height e.g. from the tree stumps	Minor to serious injury	All	1	5	5	Adult supervision of fallen big tree and stump at all times by an identified adult Children encouraged to manage their own risk and not be pushed to climb or scramble when not feeling comfortable to do so Safety checks of the site prior to session to identify any new hazards, e.g. slippery due to wet conditions	Session leader

Eating poisonous/unknown flora or fauna	Minor to serious injury	All	1	5	5	Safety talk given before entering the site – clear expectations about not ingesting anything unless given as 'authorised snack' Everyone will be made aware of the dangers and staff will make hand washing facility available for each child to clean hands before snack/drink time if provided during the session If any child ingests an unknown plant or fungi then they will return to the main school building their parents will be contacted and the medical services will be contacted for advice. All children to thoroughly wash their hands after outdoor exploring sessions – adult supervision for this to ensure thorough cleansing	Session leader
Behaviour	Minor to serious injury	Children	1	5	5	Children to be reminded of the outdoor exploring rules regarding behaviour Children must be able to demonstrate their understanding and knowledge of safe behaviour in particular situations, e.g. when building dens, etc.	Session leader

Assessor:	
Job title: Session leader (voluntary)	**Signed by Head of Establishment / Manager:**
Date of assessment:	**Date:**
Review date:	

1 This pro-forma has been adapted from www.chigwellrow.essex.sch.uk/forest_school_risk_assessments.htm (accessed 14th June 2013)

Example of an outdoor exploring briefing guide for parents

An introduction to outdoor exploring

At XXX School your child will be given the opportunity to participate in weekly outdoor explorer sessions. The purpose of this letter is to:

- provide you with some background information on outdoor exploring;
- explain why the school believes these sessions are so important;
- explain how your child will be kept safe during the sessions;
- explain what clothing will be needed.

What is outdoor exploring?

At XXX school we are fortunate to have a wilderness area located within the school grounds, which we have fenced off to provide a special place for children to explore, under adult supervision, on a regular basis. The outdoor explorer sessions focus on the **process** of learning – it is not outdoor teaching (although it may be linked to the children's classroom-based learning), rather it is an opportunity for children to regularly explore a natural setting over a prolonged period of time in small groups with high adult : child ratios. The children are given the freedom to explore the site in whatever ways they choose under the supervision of experienced staff. The sessions are predominantly child-led and so every session will be unique, with the children attending all year round (so the right clothing is particularly important!)

Why is outdoor exploring so important?

The children are provided with opportunities to regularly access the site in small groups and are given the freedom to explore and play in whatever ways they choose **under experienced adult supervision**. The sessions are therefore not about a series of planned activities, rather they provide opportunities for children and adults to co-explore in a natural outdoor setting. The wilderness area of the school playing field is central to providing this exciting approach to learning because it provides a dynamic environment with a range of sights, sounds, smells and textures that children can explore throughout the year. The site has a fenced boundary to the rear (the school's boundary fencing) and both a fence and natural boundary at the front (composed of recently planted hedging), with padlocked entrance, therefore offering a secure location to support the children's explorations. In particular, by participating in these sessions your child/children will be provided with a natural space and freedom to establish their own learning goals, to work independently and/or as part of a team, to learn new skills and to make their own personal connections with nature.

Safety

The safety of the children and accompanying adults to outdoor explorer sessions is of paramount importance. The session leaders, X & Y are both experienced in taking children outdoors; they are DBS-checked and hold current outdoor first aid and food hygiene certification. X currently works as a Teaching Assistant at the school and Y is a volunteer and a parent to one of the children attending the school. The site is safety assessed on a regular basis and safety checks take place before each session. Up-to-date risk assessments for activities the children may wish to engage in, e.g. pond dipping, den building, etc. have been completed and are regularly reviewed. A comprehensive outdoor first aid kit is always available on site and if a fire is built, additional first aid and safety equipment will be taken to the site. The school has detailed plans in case of an emergency on site and the session leaders and any accompanying adults are fully briefed on these procedures. Children are made aware of the outdoor explorer rules, which will help maintain appropriate, safe behaviour for exploring in an outdoor setting.

If you have any queries or concerns about outdoor exploring safety please contact the Head teacher.

Clothing requirements

Outdoor explorer sessions will operate year-round. In cases where there are particularly poor weather conditions that may raise safety concerns (e.g. during high winds), the session will be rescheduled.

During the winter months it is an expectation that all children and adults attending outdoor explorer sessions will come with the following clothing:

- warm hat and gloves
- jacket/waterproof coat
- waterproof over-trousers
- trousers (not school uniform)
- long-sleeved warm top (not school uniform) and layers as appropriate to the temperature
- wellington boots/sturdy outdoor shoes
- warm socks
- a spare set of warm clothes

In the warmer months, children and adults will need to have the following clothing and personal equipment:

- sun hat (preferably one that also covers the ears and neck)
- sunblock
- a thin, long-sleeved top
- trousers
- wellington boots/sturdy outdoor shoes
- waterproof jacket

If you have any questions about these sessions please contact the Head teacher

Example permissions letter to parents[1]

Dear Parent/Guardian,

I am delighted to be able to offer the Year X children the opportunity to participate in the school's new outdoor explorer sessions. Every week the children will visit an enclosed area of the school's playing fields, which have been especially developed into a natural exploring site over the past twelve months. The children will attend for a minimum 60 minute session in groups of no more than 16 with an experienced outdoor explorer session leader and adult helpers.

I am very excited to be able to offer your child this opportunity to explore our new site and to experience this exciting approach to learning. We believe that it will provide a dynamic outdoor environment for your child to explore a range of sights, sounds, smells and textures throughout the year. If you would like to find out more about what happens during an outdoor exploring session then please join me and our session leaders for a Parent Information Meeting on [date]. If you are unable to attend this meeting but would like to find out more about outdoor exploring please contact me [address below].

Outdoor exploring sessions will take place year round and will only be postponed in the event of a health & safety issue (e.g. high winds; lightning etc.). It is therefore very important that your child is appropriately dressed. The school recommends the following clothing for the cooler months:

- warm hat and gloves
- jacket/waterproof coat
- waterproof over-trousers
- trousers (not school uniform)
- long-sleeved warm top (not school uniform) and layers as appropriate to the temperature
- wellington boots/sturdy outdoor shoes
- warm socks
- a spare set of warm clothes

In the warmer months, children will need to have the following clothing and personal equipment:

- sun hat (preferably one that also covers the ears and neck)
- sunblock
- a thin, long-sleeved top
- trousers
- wellington boots/sturdy outdoor shoes
- waterproof jacket

Whilst we are at the site we will be taking lots of photos and videos of things the children do and make for you to see in our regular school newsletters. I would therefore be very grateful if you would please return the permissions slip to your child's teacher by [date].

Yours faithfully,

Head teacher

Please complete and return to your child's teacher by [date]	Please tick as appropriate	
	Yes	No
I give permission for my child [insert name] to attend the outdoor exploring sessions in Year [insert year]		
I will keep my child's teacher informed of any changes in medical information and emergency contact details		
I agree to my child receiving emergency medical treatment		
I agree to my child being photographed for training, educational and publicity purposes, including the school's website and other appropriate educational websites		
I agree to my child being videoed for training, educational and publicity purposes, including the school's website and other appropriate educational websites		

Parent/Guardian Signature: **Date:**

1 Drafted by Dr Anne Crook and adapted from the Health and Safety Guidance provided by the Oxfordshire Forest School Service, April 2013.

Examples of outdoor exploring activity risk assessments

OUTDOOR EXPLORING ACTIVITY RISK ASSESSMENT

Activity: Den Building

Identify the hazards (anything that can cause harm):

- Heavy sticks/dead branches falling
- Collapse of structure
- Blackthorn thorns/stinging nettles/thistles
- Sticks falling on feet/trapping fingers/poked in the eyes
- Injuries sustained when transporting logs/branches to the den-building site

Who might be harmed and how?	**Estimate Risk Level (H/M/L) now**
All	Medium

What measures are in place to reduce the risk?	**Estimate Risk Level now**
• The children have opportunities to learn about different ways to build dens to help them understand and manage the risks, e.g. to make sure they use appropriate sizes of branch to minimise the chance of the structure collapsing • Adult supervision whilst the den is being built and when the children are in the den • Children are taught how to safely carry sticks and logs to avoid injuring themselves or another person	Low

What further action is needed to reduce the risk? (State actions)	**Specify dates**
• Regular inspection of trees and branches above the area where den building is done • Tree inspection by a certified Tree Surgeon every 2 years	Next tree inspection is due in XXX

Assessor:	**Signed by Head of Establishment / Manager:**
Job title: Session leader (voluntary)	**Date:**
Date of assessment:	
Review date:	

OUTDOOR EXPLORING ACTIVITY RISK ASSESSMENT

Activity: Pond dipping and exploring around the pond area

Identify the hazards (anything that can cause harm):

- Slips, trips and falls
- Risk of drowning
- Stinging nettles/thistles
- Ingestion of pond water
- Injury caused by pond dipping nets (e.g. poking someone in the eye)

Who might be harmed and how?	**Estimate Risk Level (H/M/L) now**
All	Medium

What measures are in place to reduce the risk?	**Estimate Risk Level now**
<ul><li>Adult supervision at all times</li><li>The pond is not deep (10–20cm depth) but a lifebuoy is situated nearby</li><li>Children are advised to either sit on their bottoms or kneel down if they wish to explore the pond</li><li>Children are advised to walk around the pond area, not run, and are informed of the various plants that inhabit the pond area and which may cause an injury, e.g. stinging nettles, thistles</li><li>Children are informed that drinking the pond water is not safe</li><li>Children are shown how to safely use the pond dipping nets to avoid injury to themselves or another person</li><li>Children are advised to wear appropriate clothing for pond dipping, including wellington boots, waterproof over-trousers etc.</li></ul>	Low

What further action is needed to reduce the risk? (State actions)	**Specify dates**
<ul><li>Regular inspection of the pond and surrounding area to ensure any trip hazards etc. are dealt with appropriately</li><li>Regular reinforcement of the pond exploring 'rules'</li></ul>	

Assessor:	**Signed by Head of Establishment / Manager:**
Job title: Session leader (voluntary)	**Date:**
Date of assessment:	
Review date:	

Explorer session clothing

Explorer sessions will take place year-round. In cases where there are inclement conditions (e.g. high winds; lightning) that may lead to health and safety issues, the session will be postponed.

During the winter months it is an expectation that all children and adults attending explorer sessions will come with the following clothing:

- warm hat and gloves
- waterproof coat
- waterproof over-trousers
- trousers (not school uniform)
- long-sleeved warm top (not school uniform) and layers as appropriate to the temperature
- wellington boots/sturdy outdoor shoes/boots
- warm socks
- a spare set of warm clothes

In the warmer months, children and adults will need to have the following clothing and personal equipment:

- sun hat (preferably one that also covers the ears and neck)
- sunblock
- a thin, long-sleeved top
- trousers
- wellington boots/sturdy outdoor shoes/boots
- waterproof jacket (in case of a summer shower)

Example of explorer session structure

The following session structure is used for EYFS children through to Key Stage 2 at our explorer site (within the school grounds):

- Assisting adults are briefed on the site safety check (conducted by the lead adult) to highlight any new hazards (e.g. caused by weather) and measures to be taken to reduce risk to individuals from those hazards. This is done in class as the children are getting dressed.
- Children get dressed, as appropriate for the local weather conditions. Younger children may require some assistance. The lead adult checks that children have appropriate clothing and spare items are found, as necessary (usually hats and gloves).
- The number of children participating in the session and any additional information about the children that may usefully inform the session is given to the lead adult and supporting adults.
- The children walk, in pairs, to the site, enter through the usual gate and sit at the log circle.
- The kit bag is placed in the usual location on the wooden bench with the first aid bag clearly visible.
- The lead adult runs through the explorer rules and checks the children's awareness of any new issues to take into consideration (e.g. slippery ground; ice). If necessary the explorer zip method is used to ensure children are listening. *This is where children are asked to imagine that they have a zip across their mouth and they must keep their zip closed whilst the explorer rules are being explained. The children raise their hand if they wish to speak, at which point, the adult allows them to open their zip.*
- "Ready, steady, explore!" – The children are now free to explore the site. Adults circulate with the lead adult conducting regular head counts.
- The tambourine signal is given at the end of the session and children reconvene at the log circle as they know that this sound means: come back to the log circle immediately.
- The lead adult does a head count.
- The leader wraps the session up; for example, by asking some questions or by summarising the range of exploring activities observed today.
- Children get back into pairs and walk back to class. The leader does a final site check to make sure no items have been left behind (particularly clothing).
- The assisting adults are responsible for ensuring the children have all thoroughly washed their hands before returning to class.

Kit list

This is a list of the kit we take out when exploring outdoors with children.

- a list of all participants in your group (children and adults) including any relevant medical information/medicines (essential);
- comprehensive first aid kit (essential). We use a St John Ambulance first aid carry kit (www.stjohnsupplies.co.uk) and add extra pieces of kit so that it contains the following items:
  - plasters (waterproof, hypoallergenic and in assorted sizes);
  - antiseptic wipes;
  - sterile eye wash in individual 20ml tubes;
  - pair of nitrile powder-free examination gloves (medium size);
  - sterile dressings in a range of sizes;
  - burns gel ('Burnshield Hydrogel');
  - emergency silver foil blanket;
  - pair of surgical scissors;
  - triangular bandage;
  - instant ice pack ('Kool Pak': single-use, disposable, no refrigeration required);
  - pop-up emergency shelter;
  - emergency survival bag.
- mobile phone or other reliable method of communication, such as walkie-talkies (essential);
- tarpaulin (at least 4m x 4m) and a set of bungee cords/small ropes to be able to make a quick shelter (essential);
- tambourine/whistle/loud horn to gather your group together and/or use to attract attention in case of emergency (essential);
- spare set of clothes (at least one full spare set appropriate to the age range of children in your group – essential if you are working at a remote site);
- notebook and pencil to make observations (essential);
- flora/fauna identification guidebooks/sheets or downloaded onto your mobile device (useful);
- camera (or tablet/smart phone) (useful);
- penknife. Many penknives will be multifunctional and their implements can be useful – e.g. tweezers to remove a splinter; knife blade to cut through rope/string (useful);
- torch. Your children may find natural holes in the ground or in logs – a torch can help them see inside to investigate. A torch may also be useful to attract attention in case of emergency in low light levels (useful).

Observation sheet template

Date Time	Group number of children : adults	Session	Weather/ conditions	Session aims	Resources/equipment used	Observations	Personal reflections

Outdoor explorer rules

1. Listen! Always return to the log circle when you hear the special sound (tambourine).
2. Look after each other, the adults and look after the animals and plants living on the site.
3. Always stay inside the explorer site boundary unless a grown up is with you.
4. Have fun!

With younger children the rules are accompanied by pictures (see Chapter 1, Figure 1.4).

There may be additional rules/advice depending on local conditions; e.g. no climbing onto the logs or felled trees on wet, icy days and extra caution near the pond when the ground nearby is slippery and/or icy.

Outdoor exploring pre-session site safety check list template[1]

Pre-planning	Yes/No	Additional comments
Has a suitable risk assessment for the site been drafted and signed by the head teacher?		
Have risk assessments been drafted and signed by the head teacher for specific outdoor exploring activities?		
Has a pre-site check been conducted to assess: • Access to the site • Boundaries • Canopy, shrub, field and ground layers • Weather • Fire pit area and surrounds • Shelters and any other structures • People and other wild/man-made factors, e.g. dogs; litter etc.		
Does the site have mobile phone reception?		
Is there a landline nearby?		
Have relevant permissions and medical information been sorted?		
Has a first aider been designated? Do adults know where the first aid kit is located on site?		
Are there sufficient numbers of adults supporting the session?		
Do the adults supporting the session have up-to-date DBS checks?		

Before going to the site	Yes/No	Additional comments
Does the session leader have a list of those attending the session and is a copy of these details available on site and in the school?		
Do the children and any supporting adults have adequate clothing for the weather and site conditions?		
Does the session leader have the following items on site: • A spare change of clothes? (appropriate to the children's age group) • First aid kit? • Emergency sterile water (eyewash)? • Any medicines etc. that may be needed by participants? • Tissues? • A charged mobile phone (and/or back-up walkie-talkies)? • Survival blanket/bag? • Snacks and drinks? (if being taken) • Bowls, towel, handwash, water? (if snacks/drinks being provided)		
During the session	**Yes/No**	**Additional Comments**
Are the first aid kit and emergency equipment visible/easily located?		
Are you regularly counting the group?		
Are you carrying out on-going risk assessments of activities, children and weather conditions?		
Are the group members sufficiently warm/cool?		
Are the physical needs of the group members being met, e.g. shelter, refreshments etc.?		

I   Adapted from the 'Health and Safety Guidance at Forest School' leaflet, Forest School Association.

Useful kit and contacts

Helen Bilton

Helen is Associate Professor in Education at the University of Reading. She has been studying and researching about the outdoor teaching and learning environment for the last 32 years. She has authored many books. Email: h.o.bilton@reading.ac.uk
  Profile: www.reading.ac.uk/education/about/staff/h-o-bilton.aspx

Anne Crook

Anne is the Educational Development Consultant (Sciences) at Oxford University. She has been studying and researching children's outdoor explorations for the past five years and is a qualified Forest School Leader.
  Email: anne.crook@learning.ox.ac.uk
  Profile: https://www.learning.ox.ac.uk/about/staff/

Useful kit

Emergency pop up shelter

An easy and inexpensive way of creating an immediate shelter. www.amazon.co.uk/Emergency-protective-emergency-instantly-required/dp/B003CZAGMW/ref=sr_1_3?ie=UTF8&qid=1421668130&sr=8-3&keywords=emergency+shelter

Emergency blanket

A blanket to use in an emergency which has a heat reflective metallic surface which will retain the heat and offer protection against the weather. www.amazon.co.uk/Steroplast-Emergency-Camping-Blanket-Hiking/dp/B0017L48RC/ref=sr_1_1?ie=UTF8&qid=1421668187&sr=8-1&keywords=emergency+blanket

Eyewash

Eye wash is a simple way of ensuring if someone does get something in their eye it can be flushed out cleanly. www.amazon.co.uk/Emergency-Sterile-Wash-5x20ml-Saline/dp/B0029S8LQG/ref=pd_bxgy_d_img_y

First aid kits

It is advisable to have a first aid kit with you and this is an example of one already made up. www.amazon.co.uk/St-John-Ambulance-Workplace-Compliant/dp/B005JRULRG/ref=sr_1_4?ie=UTF8&qid=1421667993&sr=8-4&keywords=st+john+first+aid+kit

Hoppa trolley

A hoppa trolley will enable you to carry everything you might need when out exploring, and it is easy to use. www.amazon.co.uk/Hoppa-Lightweight-Collapsible-Groceries-Drawstring/dp/B00FMVD3KG/ref=sr_1_1?ie=UTF8&qid=1421668227&sr=8-1&keywords=hoppa+shopping+trolley

Waterproof backpacks

Waterproof back packs to use whatever the weather. www.amazon.co.uk/WATERPROOF-LTR-PREMIUM-BACKPACK-YELLOW/dp/B001FOQT4Q/ref=sr_1_5?ie=UTF8&qid=1421667924&sr=8-5&keywords=waterproof+rucksack

Useful contacts and websites

British Broadcasting Corporation (BBC)

The BBC website has a wealth of information, one of which is the Nature wildlife site and includes, for example, a section on fungi: www.bbc.co.uk/nature/life/Fungus#intro www.bbc.com/earth/uk

Council for Learning Outside the Classroom (CLOtC)

This is described as a national voice for learning outside the classroom, which offers resources and advice and has an accreditation scheme for schools. www.lotc.org.uk/

Forestry Services Commission (FSC)

The Forestry Commission's mission is to protect and expand forests and woodlands and increase their value to society and the environment. Your local Forestry Commission can be a source of logs and bark chippings: www.forestry.gov.uk/

Freecycle

Freecycle is a network of local groups who give away things for free: www.freecycle.org

Gumtree

Gumtree has some free resources, including natural resources such as logs, trees, and hay bales: www.gumtree.com/freebies/uk/trees+for+sale   www.gumtree.com/for-sale/uk/hay+bales and also items to buy such as willow and bamboo.

Health and Safety Executive (HSE)

The HSE's mission is the prevention of death, injury and ill health to those at work and those affected by work activities. This organisation talks in terms of common sense approach to health and safety and there is a very useful site about this approach in schools: www.hse.gov.uk/services/education/sensible-leadership/index.htm

The organisation argues that play is important for children's well – being and development and that careful consideration should be given to risk, the benefits of risky activities and acknowledges that accidents may happen. The HSE has worked with the Play Safety Forum to produce a joint high-level statement that gives clear messages tackling misunderstandings around health and safety and children.

Project Wild Thing

Project Wild Thing is a film led movement to get more children outside and reconnecting with nature. The film is a feature-length documentary that takes a funny and revealing look at a complex issue, the increasingly disparate connection between children and nature. http://projectwildthing.com/

St John's Ambulance

For first aid advice and help. www.sja.org.uk/sja/default.aspx

The Royal Society for the Projection of Birds (RSPB)

The RSPB is a member of BirdLife International, a partnership of conservation organisations working to give nature a home around the world. It is a useful source of information, including for example guidance on when to feed birds: www.rspb.org.uk/makeahomeforwildlife/advice/helpingbirds/feeding/whentofeed.aspx www.rspb.org.uk/

The Royal Society for the Prevention of Accidents (RoSPA)

RoSPA promote safety and the prevention of accidents at work, at leisure, on the road, in the home and through safety education. This is a particularly useful organisation when thinking about play and children and what to consider to keep children safe but it also shows how to be objective when thinking about safety. www.rospa.com/

The Woodland Trust

The Woodland Trust is the UK's largest woodland conservation charity and they remain at the forefront of the fight to protect, plant and restore UK woodland. They have lots of guidance and resources to support outdoor exploration, including nature detectives: www.naturedetectives.org.uk/ which offers games and activities for use outside. www.woodlandtrust.org.uk/

Index